It's Just Politics:

How Donald Trump beat Hillary Clinton and a review of 10 other historical Presidential campaigns.

Graham W. Milton, Jr.

DEDICATION

To all who voted – thank you.

Table of Contents

ACKNOWLEDGMENTS

To our founding fathers for creating a democracy that allows for both passionate debate and peaceful transfer of power, we thank you.

Any mistakes are the authors alone. Please send corrections or comments to gwmiltonjr@gmail.com with the Subject: 'It's Just Politics'.

Thank you.

INTRODUCTION

What an incredible, shocking but not stunning outcome! As I lay awake receiving occasional pings from my partner, daughters and friends, it became obvious that 2016 would be an historic election – one that will forever go down as the most contentious and disruptive in American history.

We did a little research and had eleven essays written about 10 of the most competitive – and combative campaigns in history. And one about the Trump – Clinton election of 2016. They are by themselves, interesting summaries of what some historians consider the worst of times when it comes to politics. The vitriol and raw emotions that they expose make us – Americans, seem like an ignorant, stupid bunch at times as the dialog is often irrational and the intellectual debates superficial.

The results of these elections by themselves provide us with a fascinating look at growth in the United States electorate – from just 16 states in 1800 with fewer than 100,000 voters to 50 states (plus the District of Columbia and U.S. territories) with over 120,000,000 voters in 2016.

These essays also show how political parties have come and gone. Federalists and Whigs, Democratic Republicans. Liberal Republicans. Democrats and Republicans. National Republicans. National Unionists.

Candidates from California and Texas, New York and Massachusetts. Ohio, Pennsylvania, Vermont, Virginia, South Dakota, and Maine too.

All men save for Ms. Clinton. All white. Many fathers, brothers, husbands. A few divorced or single. Some allegedly had affairs. Others were known to have.

And as a result of some of these elections and their lingering aftermaths, laws and policies and positions were changed sometimes quite dramatically. From Constitutional amendments, to post Civil War Reconstruction; from term limits to how candidates are nominated. The process continues to evolve over time.

All in the pursuit of what is arguably the most powerful position in human history. President of the United States of America.

In reviewing these essays, there are a few things we conclude:

- Parties, rules, and laws change over time.

- Negative campaigning is not new.

- How information gets out to the 'masses' has changed dramatically.

Until a hundred years ago, news was shared verbally in speeches, or person to person or via the written word in pamphlets, books, newspapers, and letters. Candidates often did not participate directly in the campaigning – leaving it to surrogates. As transportation and high ways improved, the reach of the candidates expanded at a faster pace. News could travel faster. A speech could be reprinted and reach a wide audience in weeks rather than months. The famous Cooper Union speech by Abraham Lincoln is one example of this as it introduced him formally to the intellectual elite in the Northeast who were previously quite suspect about this 'rail splitter' from Illinois.

And then radio allowed a person to communicate with many more potential voters across great distances audibly. Franklin Roosevelt used the radio to warm the hearts of depression and World War II era voters making the electorate feel more in touch with their disabled leader. And when television entered the scene it had a somewhat dramatic impact on presidential elections as was seen in the famous Kennedy/Nixon debates in 1960. Finally, today, we live in a world with no bounds as news and information is available in a variety of forms as it happens. So a candidate can tweet what they think, when they think it to as many followers as they have.

We live in an era of citizen journalism where with our smart phones and an internet connection we can broadcast live anything we see or think anytime of the day or night and reach a global audience.

Enter Negative Campaigning

What these 10 essays show is that running a negative campaign is not new. The harsh words and tactics of Trump are direct ancestors of the vitriol and actions of Jefferson, Adams, Jackson amongst others.

One study showed how that negative campaigning actually worked[1]. The researchers explained that negative political campaigns had more impact on Democrats than it had on Republicans.

Hardcore Republicans were found to vote for their preferred candidate even if that candidate had been portrayed in bad light. In contrast, Democrats were found to be influenced to shy away from voting or to switch allegiance altogether. The study's conclusion was that Republican candidates benefited more from negative ad peddling than their Democratic counterparts. This study seems to vindicate the presidential election of 1872 – and Trumps victory in 2016.

Another aspect of campaigning is how the candidates can minimize the sometimes dramatic impact of truly bad news by inoculating their followers against attacks from the other party.

---

[1] See Ansolabehere, S. & Iyengar, S. (1995). Going negative: How campaign advertising shrinks and polarizes the electorate. New York: The Free Press as an example.

We see this in these campaigns as each candidate tries to outdo each other – not necessarily by making themselves seem better or more moral, but instead by making the other candidate seem worse.

In comparison to what has already been said or done, any new 'nasty' stuff will seem minor. Consider the impact of the recording of Trump and Billy Bush discussing how he engages women. Because of the previous information and Trumps rampant denial, we forgive his words and presumed actions. We have – in affect, been inoculated against the bad stuff because of the heavy intense negative campaigning that has already taken place. And this is exactly what the campaign managers want: An electorate who doesn't care how nasty or bad their candidate might be.

Other observations.

The 10 historical campaigns also reviewed each had defining actions that built the foundation for today's campaigns. You can see it in cartoons and caricatures derived from Thomas Nast's famous attacks on Journalist Horace Greeley in 1872.

Party in-fighting is also nothing new. Even our founding fathers were not immune to the nasty tactics of some of the very people that they had fought for independence with as can be seen in the election of 1800 that led to a constitutional change.

As much as we like to think Trump was a one of a kind candidate, consider that Thomas Jefferson had people referring to him as a philanderer, and adulterer. He was hated, and the people were told that electing him as the President would lead to a breakdown in society.

Electing a business man, as opposed to a career politician or lawyer is also nothing new. We've had actors, journalists, military men, shop keepers, and even an owner of a haberdashery. Our presidents have been disabled, dealt with depression, and a wide variety of other ailments. Our presidents have been athletes, they have been married, divorced, and single. We've also had fathers and sons.

Of course all have been male. And all except for President Obama have been white.

What we hope is that this contribution will shed light on our history. We hope that these short essays inspire you to dig deeper, find out more information, learn about our history. We also hope that it gets you thinking about the people we elect as we try to sort through the effects of the 2016 campaign and election of Donald Trump as our President and the good and the bad that can come of it.

  - *Graham W. Milton, Jr*. Hartford. December 2, 2016.

2016

CHAPTER 1: How Trump Beat Clinton

DONALD TRUMP VS. HILLARY CLINTON

| ***Donald Trump*** | ***Hillary Clinton*** |

---

[2]By Michael Vadon - →This file has been extracted from another file: Donald Trump August 19, 2015.jpg, CC BY-SA 2.0, https://commons.wikimedia.org/w/index.php?curid=42609338
[3] By Gage Skidmore, CC BY-SA 3.0, https://commons.wikimedia.org/w/index.php?curid=46897599

How Trump Won

From the moment he stood on an escalator at Trump Tower in New York to make an announcement to a group of journalists, Donald J. Trump had already mapped out a plan for a race that would take only 18-months or so, but that would undoubtedly leave America thrilled – or at least insulted – before the now president-elect had spoken his message.

This is what it looked like to the neutral observer; but in the subsequent months the U.S. electoral process underwent a contentious, hate-filled campaign that has catapulted the real estate magnate into global leadership and stirred up the ruling class in a way not seen before. What surprised the corporates and early skeptics was the way in which Trump's message of "putting America first" and his promises to repeal existing immigration and tax laws appealed to the blue-collar population.

Perhaps if Trump had run a more conventional campaign – and managed a lead on the polls long before Election Day, his triumph would have come to be only a surprising event and not something that resembled a shocking work of fiction. But Trump's campaign has been loaded with scandal and controversy from start to finish.

An unusual candidacy

Let's step back to when Trump announced his candidacy in 2015. As a matter of fact, he had already launched a presidential exploratory committee back in 2011 and visited a few key battleground states before pulling out: it hadn't been the right time. But in 2015, from the iconic Trump Tower, *the Donald* announced to the press, his supporters and everyone nearby, that he was "officially running for President of the United States." Prior to the announcement, the pundits had concluded that he would never run, mainly given that he was a very private man and would never acquiesce to the scrutiny and reporting that typically follows presidential candidates.

It was easy to pass off Trump's announcement that he was seeking a Republican nomination for president as a joke or publicity stunt, but as we've come to see, national politics creates an environment that seems to favor celebrity personas, and therefore the TV personality was bound to get all the attention in the media.

Not everybody liked to see his name in all the news headlines, but that distaste was also part of the reason his name was there in the first place. Considering the comical way in which many people viewed his announcement, one would've expected Trump to follow up with serious political speeches at his rallies; not the sensational, factually-incorrect assertions that he made in the subsequent months. But he was getting free press, and he was going to define the campaign narrative no matter what it took.

After his announcement in New York, the Democratic National Committee issued a tongue-in-cheek statement summing up his participation in the process as someone who "adds much-needed seriousness that has been lacking in the GOP field." The DNC was looking to hear more about his ideas for the nation. Of course, some of these ideas included building a great wall along the U.S.-Mexico border and invalidating the

Affordable Care Act (or "Obamacare") along with a number of international trade agreements.

For a presidential aspirant to call one of the major minority groups in the country "rapists" and "drug dealers" sets a bad tone for the rest of the campaign and severely distracted from the real issues. However, Trump sailed through the ensuing months with a degree of smugness and misogyny – so much so that by the time he was the Republican nominee, many people and pundits were left to wonder how the U.S. general election had descended so low.

Republican nomination

Trump's seizure of the Republican nomination came out of a record-breaking primaries turnout. The Republican Party's pre-convention state election turnout had over 28 million votes – which is 139% higher than the turnout in 2008. Trump had more wins than any Republican candidate with 33 primary wins. He also funded his own primary campaign – the first candidate to do so in the modern era.

In a speech describing his primary win, Trump went on to thank his supporters for the 13 million raw votes he received and talked about how he managed to beat a rigged system thanks to "overwhelming support." Trump was quick to boast about the "movement" he inspired and how that had translated into millions of votes; and this was largely backed by statistical data. For instance, turnout was up by 11 million ballots in the Republican primaries compared to 2012, even though the eligible voter group had only grown by about 5 million.

But was "Trump-love" responsible for the high Republican vote bonanza? Not exactly. As it happens, voter turnout was high across the board, even in states that didn't support him; this suggests that anti-Trump sentiment was just as effective in drawing people out to vote – at least during the primaries. And perhaps foretelling the results of the general election, even though Trump managed to claim a majority of delegates in the primaries, he only got a relatively small share of the GOP primaries' popular vote.

But this was, of course, due to competition. When Trump began his campaign for the nomination, the Republican Party had 17 aspirants. That number quickly narrowed down to a three-way race – or to be more accurate, to a two-way duel between the most popular candidates: Donald Trump and Ted Cruz.

In 2012, Mitt Romney had spent the better part of four months going back and forth with Ron Paul and New Gingrich before finishing with a majority of the popular vote. Fast-forward to 2016, and most of Trump's rivals had dropped out two months in, leaving him to battle it out with just one obvious threat: Ted Cruz.

This still wasn't in any way an indication of Trump's eventual rise to power, because if the Democrat's popular vote is to be considered, Hillary Clinton already had a solid head start, and in fact appeared to be the favorite throughout the campaign.

Controversy

From his first comments on the steps of Trump Tower questions of whether Donald Trump had "gone too far" kept popping up. His problem with female voters started early as his message was said not to resonate with college-educated females; and as his campaign gained momentum, more women started coming out with damning confessions. Indeed, Trump's inability to gain support among young female voters was seen as a major impediment to his campaign and a thing that would derail his efforts. This did not happen and throughout the revelations, Trump was not willing to empathize or apologize.

But things didn't quite go as expected, and the Trump campaign was punctuated by dozens of shockingly offensive episodes. As the campaign kicked off, Trump went on to shout, insult, steamroll, and bully his way to become a major presidential nominee – in fact, the presidential nominee of the party of Abraham Lincoln.

Throughout the campaign Trump showed outrageous behavior and made offensive statements regarding every sensitive political issue of the day. Some of his statements alienated African American voters, Mexicans, Muslims, and disabled people; and while in any normal election such volatile issues would have disqualified him, Trump had already bagged most of his supporters.

It was his role as an outsider that resonated with voters, not his temperament. He came out of the gate challenging the establishment and demanding change in the status quo and some much-needed consideration for the average American. As he pressed for higher control of our borders and addressed economic concerns affecting blue-collar types, he carefully set himself apart as the only candidate that was looking out for the voter. Whenever he went off-script and insulted people or made wild, false accusations, his supporters excused him and were quick to point out that he's "not a politician", but instead a real estate brawler who made a fortune counter-punching.

Perhaps no other controversy than the October leak of Trump's lewd comments about women from 2005 as just one of the countless disturbing revelations about him showed how loyal his supporters were. They didn't seem to to care about any of the controvery's. And there were many – especially with regards to women. The following are a few of the controversies regarding women that were highlighted during his campaign:

July 2015

Just one month after Trump announced his run for president, an old divorce deposition involving his first wife, Ivana, surfaced. In it she described an encounter with Trump in the late 1980s as "rape", something Trump's lawyers were quick to counter. Michael Cohen, special counsel for the Trump Organization, stated that one cannot be accused of "raping" one's spouse. "There's very clear case law", he said.

August 2015

During the Republican presidential debate, Fox News anchor and moderator Megyn Kelly questioned Trump about his insults of women, recalling that he had used terms like "fat pigs" and "slobs" to describe them. But Trump was quick to respond, "Only Rosie O'Donnell". He was referring to a decade-long feud between the two media personalities.

Around the same time, an article on Rolling Stone revealed how Trump had mocked Carly Fiorina's appearance during an incident when she was on the news. "Look at that face!" he growled as the camera panned to Fiorina, former CEO of Hewlett Packard and then-presidential aspirant. "Would anyone vote for that?"

December 2015

During a debate rally with Democratic candidate Hillary Clinton, Trump made vulgar comments about his contender. "I know where she went – it's disgusting, I don't want to talk about it." He was talking about a restroom break Hillary Clinton had taken during the event. Trump also referenced her 2008 Democratic primary loss to Barack Obama, and used a vulgar term.

"She was favored to win, and she got schlonged," Trump said.

January 2016

Former Trump Organization staffer Mae Davidson alleged that she and her female colleagues were paid less than their male counterparts. She also said that Trump had once commented on her and a female colleague's appearance, saying, "You guys could do a lot of damage." Trump's campaign was quick to refute the claims and added that Davidson had been fired for "doing a terrible job."

April 2016

Trump accused Clinton of using "the woman card", which prompted the Clinton campaign team to start brandishing the term and made it a talking point in some of their rallies.

May 2016

In a report by the New York Times, scores of women came out to say that Trump had made unwanted advances on them. The women included former pageant contestants, employees, and companions of Trump.

September 2016

During the first presidential debate, Hillary Clinton detailed Trump's treatment of Alicia Machado, former beauty queen. Trump was accused of calling the woman

"Miss Piggy" and "Miss Housekeeping" because of weight-gain and the fact that she is Latina.

At his California gold club, Trump was accused of wanting to fire hostesses that he felt weren't pretty enough.

November 2016

Just days before the election, new reports surfaced alleging that Melania Trump had worked illegally in the U.S., taking on modeling contracts before she was issued a visa from the United States government. The Associated Press released documents that they claimed indicated that Melania obtained at least ten modeling jobs (worth $20,056) in the seven weeks before she had legal permission to seek employment in the country.

The claim was particularly embarrassing for Trump, who had premised his campaign on tough immigration and threatened to deport millions of unauthorized workers. He has since argued for thorough analysis of the status of immigrants in the country to find out whether they can be allowed to work.

His dismissal of the lewd comments made behind-the-scenes at a recording session as "locker room banter" did not calm the storm of controversy that surrounded his campaign. In fact, they were described by some experts as "the straw that will break the camel's back".

The Election

Virtually every news source, pollster, experienced politician expected Hillary Clinton would win the popular vote by between 2 and 4% points. And she did end up winning the popular vote by over 2,000,000 – or over 2%.

As the clock ticked toward 2:30 AM on November 9th, it was clear she had lost. At 2:39 AM, on November 9th, Hillary Clinton called Donald Trump to concede defeat. It was probably one of the most difficult calls of her life, and the fact that she had to do it was one of the most surprising turns in a political process full of surprises.

The popular vote, while important does not determine the winner of a presidential election. The Electoral College does.

The Electoral College is made up of 538 electors (1 for each congressman and senator per state plus 3 for the District of Columbia) who cast their votes to decide who the President and Vice President of the United States will be. When people vote, they vote to choose the candidate that will receive the electors votes. A candidate must win 270 electoral college votes to win the election.

Our founding fathers established the Electoral College as a compromise between having the people and congress vote for the President. Legally, the electors do not have to vote for the candidate who wins the majority of the popular vote in their state. And sometimes they don't.

Five times candidates have lost the popular vote and won the Presidency:

1824 – John Quincy Adams

1876 – Rutherford B. Hayes

1888 – Benjamin Harrison

2000 – George W. Bush

2016 – Donald Trump

Over the past decade or so, the Republicans have cleverly figured out how to get a majority of governors, representatives, and senators elected despite having a clear demographic disadvantage.

The 2016 Presidential election showed how a candidate can target specific states and groups of people and win leveraging the Electoral College and ignoring the popular vote.

Really what Trump and Richard Priebus (Chairman of the Republican National Committee), and the team who helped get him elected did was to find out what got people excited – excited enough to actually vote on November 8th – or before hand.

With negative rating higher even than Hillary Clinton, it is truly phenomenal that Donald Trump still won. But he did. So who voted for him?

The white, working-class voter

By the time Trump won the GOP nomination, the working class had already started to gravitate towards him. Trump viewed Hillary Clinton as the personification of everything that is wrong with Washington. He made a connection between what he called a "rigged system, a gridlock of bureaucracy that is all-talk and no action". His message was that his opponent was more than only Hillary; she was a symbol of the failing system.

When the surge of Bernie Sanders supporters hit the Clinton campaign, it seemed to catch her unaware – much like her 2008 defeat by Barack Obama – and the Trump campaign knew her path wasn't certain. The Clinton narrative had already sunk in. She was defined as "crooked", and as someone that people should mistrust and dislike. Trump's campaign just needed to keep hammering this message in whenever her name was mentioned.

When the Trump campaign started lashing out with terms like "Crooked Hillary" and "drain the swamp," they were repeating slogans that had been repeated by

Republican conservatives for over 20 years, but that had not stu ck until now. Hillary didn't come off as someone who took risk, and this led many to question her entire campaign and the notion that she could be a president who would bring about change.

Trump saw something the other party missed: a growing discontent among the white working class. The polls put Clinton ahead of Trump, and the traditional view of American elections helped lull the Democrats into a false sense of security. National exit polls had showed that Barack Obama won the 2012 election without much support from the white voters – they had suggested that a Democrat candidate hadn't been as unpopular with white voters since Walter Mondale.

This was interpreted to mean that a Democrat candidate faced no major losses, especially once a white candidate replaced Obama: but of course the truth was that Democrats were hugely dependent on white working-class voters. Exit polls tend to overlook the importance of this demographic to Democrats and, in general, overestimate the number of well-educated non-white voters.

For the last few decades, America's blue-collar white men had to put up with dwindling paychecks and a total devaluing of their work. Factories and mines and shops were closed down, affecting the livelihood of many communities across the heart of America; and what happened next didn't help change the course of events.

New factories popped up in cities where they didn't live, with college-educated staffers. Currently, large populations across the U.S. feel left behind and are pessimistic about a rapidly globalizing economy. These frustrations did not go unnoticed to Donald Trump as he traveled the country talking to farmers and regular business owners.

These people rejected the business-friendly policies that have been implemented by elites in both parties, along with their deepening trade relationships with foreign countries and their promotion of immigration. This trend of rising inequality and major economic dislocation was starting to define America in ways that some leaders were failing to notice.

The total number of white voters without a college degree in the 2016 electorate stood at about a third. Trump won 39% of them, surpassing 2012 Republican nominee Mitt Romney, who had won 25%. These individuals were the foundation of Trump's victories; particularly in the Rust Belt region, including the blowout win in Ohio and major upsets in Wisconsin and Pennsylvania.

This block of voters had expressed deep-seated racial and cultural anxieties and were shown to be in support of deporting illegal immigrants; however, it should be noted that the same polls also suggested that economic concerns and hostility towards lenders were some of the more serious issues driving them to Trump.

Half of working-class voters mentioned the economy as the most vital issue, and 14% mentioned immigration. Most of them said that foreign trade is responsible for taking away American jobs.

These frustrations aren't exactly new; they have been brewing for years, boiling over in the recovery from the Great Recession. In the period from 1975 to 2014, white male workers without a college degree saw a reduction in median income by 20%, and their incomes dropped by 14% between 2007 and 2014.

As a result of a growing U.S. economy, their incomes increased by about 6% last year, but that still hasn't made up the difference when you count the last recession – let alone the 1970s. These struggling working-class voters had not seen the fruits of American prosperity. While "Superstar" cities like Boston, Washington, and San Francisco attracted wealth over the years, they were left to stagnate in small cities and rural areas where businesses continued to fold and job opportunities were dwindling.

When a large portion of the population feels as if their access to economic opportunity comes down to geographic luck, there's bound to be hostility towards the ruling class. These regions have gradually lost factory jobs as trade expansion and high technology pushes the economy away from production and into service, as with the closing of coal mines. In fact, according to the United State Bureau of Labor Statistics, over 1,000,000 manufacturing jobs have been lost since 1980 – 15 years before the North American Free Trade Agreement went into effect. There was a period of hope as the lucrative energy-extraction support jobs, but even those opportunities disappeared when oil prices fell.

These are some of the reasons for why most of these workers came to see trade deals as a bad thing, especially the North American Free Trade Agreement that includes Canada and Mexico, and the trade deal with China (signed in 2000) which some economic researchers suggest may have cost America 2 million jobs.

A Gift from God

Trump rallied his supporters amongst the working class population, promising to restore the old industrial economy by negotiating import tariffs and trade deals and by deporting scores of immigrants, which is meant to reduce competition for native-born workers. He also talked about rapid economic growth, which he said would be spurred by deregulation, drilling, and significant tax cuts.

There were warnings from economists who suggested that Trump's plans will not deliver those promises to desperate workers. Clinton's supporters also argued that tariffs can't bring back jobs and could, in fact, lead to another recession. But his supporters didn't trust anything coming out of Washington, and nobody was going to take away the one chance they had at a political revolution. They saw Trump as the answer to a problem that had been festering for years.

Trump saw the success he had in the primaries' rallies and saw no need to change his tactic. The message had gotten through; he only needed to expand beyond the base he had created in the primaries and perhaps bring in a few establishment types. Speeches and presentations were the way to do this, and policy would be discussed at length over the teleprompter.

Every single one of his voters believed that Trump represents a change. The question is: what kind of change?

Trump's Message

Trump copied and recast an old Reagan promise to "make America great again": just four words that seemed to capture both hope and fear, optimism and pessimism – appealing to the heart, not the head. His audiences ate it up as he expounded more on their struggles with economic opportunity, making sure to fault the existing leadership for what he called "a history of terrible mistakes".

The massive support for Trump, despite all his flaws and controversies, displayed the strong feelings that Americans have –that they feel like the country has been let down by poor leadership and misplaced corporate and global interests. From their standpoint, leaders didn't look at issues like immigration properly; when they regulated immigration, it wasn't to the American laborer's advantage, and trade was leveraged against the common businessman.

Their support for Trump was a way of expressing deep discontent and betrayal, a conviction so strong that it completely overwhelmed all controversy.

TV Personality

Trump's role as host of The Apprentice provided him with a 10-year platform of being in front of the TV as boss, CEO, dealmaker and employer, famously firing people and being the bold entrepreneur who can fix things. This role of an authoritarian patriarchal magnate led millions of people across the country to see him as a "trustworthy" individual, and that undoubtedly translated into millions of votes from all demographics.

In this media age, Trump had begun by accumulating major financial and celebrity capital, and he put it to use. His opponent, on the other hand, was a candidate whose unpopularity rating was only surpassed by Trumps. Clinton, as the wife of a former president and running to succeed a two-term Democrat, was the ultimate face of the establishment and therefore everything that's wrong in America. The lack of enthusiasm for her candidacy compared to Barack Obama's in 2008 was palpable, and that vulnerability was further highlighted when she struggled to beat a 74-year old socialist from Vermont during the Democratic primaries.

Voters had unconsciously positioned themselves as enemies of the establishment, and now perceived themselves to be caught in an economic downdraft – believing their children would be worse off than they had been – and as a result, they wanted a major fix.

It didn't help that Clinton's political career was loaded with baggage, most notably the FBI investigation into her use of a private email server during her tenure as secretary of state. And in late October, when the FBI said it had uncovered a new batch of emails, the whiff of scandal raised earlier in the year persisted despite Hillary's assertion that there was nothing to find in the investigation and that she had only "made a mistake" in using the server. The subject was constantly rehashed in virtually all of Trump's rallies and the message that Hillary couldn't be trusted eventually got through to the majority of voters.

OutsiderTrump declared war on his own party, calling out the Bush family, House speaker Paul Ryan, and former nominees including John McCain and Mitt Romney. His supporters relished his attacks on the party establishment and it fueled a growing grumble that Republican members of Congress had failed to keep their promises. So when party members condemned Trump, it only served to validate him as a rallying point for his growing support group.

Those factors helped him play the role of a maverick outsider set to march against a lazy, do-nothing Washington. And yet, Trump wasn't facing criticism from the entire party establishment. As a matter of fact, Chairman Reince Priebus was quick to promote Trump as the nominee even when at times he had to twist and turn and basically excuse every new misdemeanor that hit the Trump campaign.

The role of media

According to data by Google, 46% of the media coverage about GOP candidates during the primaries was about Trump. Other Republican candidates noticed the slant in media coverage and were frustrated by it, but there was no way of stopping the Donald once he had established the media as his most powerful tool in the development of his campaign.

As one article in the Washington Post put it: "No one wakes up one morning and decides on their own that Donald Trump should be the Republican nominee for president." They get there after following a relentless bombardment of news stories about Trump.

His method was simple: make outlandish comments that will be covered on all news channels and go viral on social media, therefore generating high levels of controversy. His rivals during the primaries were delivering serious, detailed policy addresses of how they would solve existing problems if elected into office, but their speeches were not covered at length – either because they were unsurprising or because they didn't quite *affect* people as much as Trump.

Most political professionals and shell-shocked "traditional" Republicans are busy analyzing what happened in order to assign blame, but the establishment media also needs to examine its behavior in what some foreigners are calling a profound national embarrassment.

A few acknowledged leaders of journalism (The NY Times, Washington Post) went on to dispense with the customary courtesies extended to anybody standing for public office, but even they had to draw a line. Following Trump's refusal to stick with facts and months of having to describe his "misstatements" and "falsehoods", these papers decided to redefine his preposterous rhetoric for what it really was: "lies".

Why does media coverage matter in an election?

People don't form political judgments in a vacuum. Citizens need information in order to make decisions, and the media plays a huge role in determining which way they swing in an election. This matters most when the nominees are starting out, because voters have very little knowledge about most of the candidates.

A 16-candidate primary is close to a "large anonymous mass," which makes it even more impactful when the media chooses to single out an individual for coverage. But Trump is a complication. To understand his position in the media, one has to go back years, to long before he decided to run. His name was a constant in media circles, and his brand was globally recognized.

As one article described him, "Trump had more than 90% name recognition when he started his campaign." In a group of relatively unknown nominees, his face was the most familiar, and so he got everyone's attention. That might help explain why both the media and the viewers found themselves clamoring for more Trump coverage.

Trump's notoriety before this election campaign does in itself reflect media attention. He's managed to spend decades in the public eye, first in New York tabloids that detailed his real estate deals and romantic exploits, and then before the whole country when he got his own reality show. He wouldn't have managed to create such a lasting brand without a major assist from the media.

Celebrities are created both by their own efforts and by the media's willingness to write about them. There's always been a symbiotic relationship between these two parties: celebrities will say and do things that generate media interest, which ultimately generate more audiences and revenue for the media outlets, and the media will increase their coverage. This leads someone like Trump to constantly unleash controversy in an effort to gain more coverage.

Bear in mind that online media differs to a large extent from print and broadcast news, and that makes it extremely difficult to monitor. You can get two different online media platforms offering completely different results based on their respective data collection strategies. But having said that, there's plenty of data to suggest that Trump received an initial peak of coverage when he made his announcement to run, and on certain days he received more than half of the mentions of all the other GOP candidates on all news features.

It continued that way for the rest of the campaign, with only a few incidents – like when Ben Carson started receiving comparable amounts of news coverage. For the period starting from August 24 2015, to September 4 2015, Trump received 78% coverage on CNN, and he dominated most evening network news coverage in the first half of 2015, (234 minutes, compared to 7 minutes for Ted Cruz) although his announcement came late in this period.

He received more coverage in the newspapers as well. According to one analysis done by the website FiveThirtyEight.com, Trump received 54% of all newspaper coverage – defined as any article that mentions a candidate's name in the title, but no other candidate.

Why did Trump receive so much coverage?

To better understand campaign news coverage, one has to look at a few key elements: the candidates, the economic incentives of airing specific news, the values of the news organization, and the decisions of viewers and readers.

Trump was, of course, very concerned about the way in which the media covered stories of him or his business. Because of this inherent need of attention, he continuously said things that give news organizations incentive to cover him.

In addition, Trump knew exactly how to align his own behavior with the values of news organizations:

what they use to determine what they air, and what they consider newsworthy.

· Novelty: he positioned himself as "different" than his opponents.

· Controversy: he would blurt out literally any form of insult when discussing serious issues.

· Conflict: he instigated feuds whenever necessary.

· Strong personality: this came naturally to him.

Most media reports indicate that Trump's coverage surged after certain controversial remarks, like his attack on Sen. John McCain's record as prisoner of war. Another spike was recorded when he called for a ban on Muslims entering the country, and when he cancelled a rally in Chicago because of protesters.

News organizations are highly competitive, and in order to keep a share of the market, they need to claim a large number of readers and viewers. Popular news networks reported a significant growth in viewership, and new executives made sure to scoop up as many new viewers as possible. This contributed to the rise of controversy during the campaign.

One fact is often overlooked when critiquing horserace journalism: readers *like* sensationalism, and will deliberately avoid a presentation or news piece discussing the "real issues" to focus on Trump's latest Twitter spat. When given the choice, citizens will gravitate towards news stories that cover campaign strategy, or to candidate biographies as opposed to policy.

This combination of factors led to a vicious news cycle. Of course the implication of Trump's coverage to the other party nominees was grim, and the fact that his personality and strategy were so closely woven into the modus operandi of modern news networks meant that he was bound to overshadow his opponents.

The role of polls

The results of the presidential election came as a major surprise – or shock – to a lot of people who were following the state and national polling, which projected

Hillary Clinton to win the election. Election forecasters were referencing opinion polls when calculating Trump's chance of winning, and they put Clinton far ahead – from anywhere between 70% and 99% probability.

They also pegged her as the favorite to win a number of battleground states, including Wisconsin and Pennsylvania, both of which were taken by Trump. But how did the polls get it so wrong?

There have been a number of popular theories about why polling data went so far off the mark. However, most people agree on one point: polls broadly underestimated the level of Trump's support across the board. All major election forecasts varied, and it was probably due to the different methods of acquiring data. Conventional telephone polls are usually combined with the more comprehensive and online probability and non-probability sample surveys, of which the majority turned out to be inaccurate. Professional pollsters are still in the process of gathering data so as to understand what exactly happened, step-by-step.

One possible reason is what pollsters call non-responsive bias. It describes a situation in which a select group of people systematically fail to respond to surveys even with equal opportunity outreach to every area of the electorate. Some of the key groups of voters – including the white without a college degree voters that Trump had targeted – are difficult to reach, making it that much harder to come up with a definitive poll figure. Also, the same frustration that this demographic had with the establishment might have led them to ignore the polls, a thing that left many of them unquestioned for the state and national surveys.

It has also been suggested that many of the people who participated in the surveys simply weren't honest about whom they planned to vote for. The media had trumpeted the "shy Trumper" hypothesis as a possible reason for a downplaying of Trump support, especially among higher-educated white voters and Hispanics. But if a large number of Trump supporters were being dishonest when talking to a live interviewer, then online surveys would be expected to reveal more truth. But this wasn't the case. Online polls were just as likely to show support for Clinton across a wide section of the voting bloc.

The method in which pollsters identified potential voters has been questioned by experts, because as things stand, we can't possibly know in advance who exactly is going to vote. So the pollsters develop a model that predicts the most likely scenario of what the electorate will look like. This isn't an accurate method, and any small difference in assumption can lead to significant differences in election predictions. As we have seen, the votes that pollsters had projected for the Rust Belt states defied many expectations – and because most of these projected voter models incorporate some measure of enthusiasm into their calculus, the depressed vote may have wreaked havoc, particularly on the Democratic side.

Pollsters are aware of the many challenges that plague their profession, and this election has only served to highlight some of those issues. America is deeply divided along racial and economic lines, and attempts to show how people will vote turn out to be guesswork: there are just too many factors to consider.

Donald Trump on Foreign Policy

Aside from cutting down expenses on the homeland, Trump pledged to review the NATO agreement and have all member countries paying their fair share. He also called for tougher relationships with China and Russia; but when it comes to how exactly Trump plans to implement some of his proposals, we are left to wonder.

Trump constantly emphasized a new set of ideas that would in effect reduce the role that America plays in the world. He proposed unilateral action, taking us away from traditional allies and working closer with our adversaries. He proposed diminishing or possibly cutting links with America's commitments on security alliances – NATO included – and other defense treaties such as the ones America has with Japan and South Korea.

Trump also indicated that he might consider pulling out of the World Trade Center, and he called the North American Free Trade Agreement the "worst trade deal ever signed". It's not clear whether he plans to honor the climate change agreement reached in Paris in 2015.

On the issue of international security, Trump is in support of nuclear proliferation and has said that allies like Saudi Arabia should be paying America for continued support. He supported the U.S.-led invasion of Iraq at the time, but strongly criticized it during his campaign, and he has said repeatedly that America "should have taken the oil" from Iraq and Libya by force.

Are Trump's proposals sincere or just campaign talk?

It's quite difficult to extrapolate any concrete plans from Trump's announcements, since he doesn't always relay facts and he hasn't been consistent. On some days he called NATO "obsolete" and concluded that America should reduce its commitments to European security; on others he wasn't so cynical, and only said that European states should make higher contributions to NATO and focus more on terrorism.

Voters believe that he will change America's approach to foreign policy. U.S. presidents enjoy unusual autonomy on foreign issues, and it's very likely that Trump would want to get to work right away, but some of his proposals are not easy to implement. For instance, the idea of taking Iraq's oil is quite challenging – the oil rests underground in a sovereign state. Also, Mexico is not likely to comply with his demand to pay for a "Great Wall."

Foreign policy is not determined by the White House alone. It is conducted by large institutions like the State Department, the Pentagon and Intelligence Agencies; and these institutions are staffed with thousands of professional career officers. Trump has only a handful of like-minded foreign policy advisers, so he will need to work closely with these agencies – and that also means staffing them with his party's own foreign policy veterans.

Trump sees the world as chaotic and inhospitable to conventional American dreams like democracy or support for international institutions; therefore, in this hostile world, the U.S must pursue its interests very narrowly and with unapologetic force. This is what he calls "America first", and some have likened this approach to his years in the competitive real estate market of New York which, as he sees it, involves making a series of deals, each divided between a winner and a loser. But foreign alliances don't quite work the same way, and if Trump believes that every interaction must end with one side suffering a humiliating loss, it might explain why he's not in support of mutually beneficial arrangements.

The Russian Factor

Throughout the campaign, Democratic party nominee Hilary Clinton drew connections between Donald Trump and Russian President Vladimir Putin, who she said was responsible for multiple cyber-attacks against American interests. But although Hillary wanted to imply a damaging association between Trump and Putin, there's no evidence that Trump is in support of Russian interests; and those who know him personally have stated emphatically that Trump will do what is good for America.

Trump stated in his rallies that he believes an easing of tensions between the U.S. and Russia is possible, but only from a position of strength; because, as he puts it,

Russian President Vladimir Putin has "absolutely no respect" for the U.S President or Washington's apologetic approach to foreign policy. "I can talk to him," he said about Putin.

So despite his vague stance on issues of policy and wider economic challenges, Trump's message resonated with voters. Remember, he didn't win the GOP primary because of his brash, improvisational manner; he won *in spite* of it.

His stances on the economy, crime, immigration, Syria, Russia and Israel all seem to take the opposite approach from what Washington has been doing over the last several years. It's a lot of change to promise the electorate, and while we can't be sure that much of it will be implemented or that it will have a positive effect, we can understand why his message just had to be different. This notion of "changing business as usual in D.C." is something that, based on the high election turnout, his voters only trusted *him* to bring about, and not a lifelong member of the establishment. Trump's message won by 52% over Hillary's 36% ratio, with a large number of voters saying that Trump described what they were feeling "very well."

The results of the election were evidence of repudiation, not only of the Democratic candidate, but also of the Obama legacy, which finds itself suddenly imperiled. "The forgotten men and women of our country will be forgotten no longer," Trump told supporters New York rally shortly after Mrs. Clinton conceded.

Away from his usual blistering rhetoric, Trump gave a subdued victory speech that sought to bind the wounds of division, calling for people to come together as one.

"Spirit" and infrastructure

In an interview with the Washington Post, Trump talked about his plans to unite the nation – particularly in the face of a rise in racial tensions. In the interview he offered two solutions: a good dose of "spirit" and jobs.

He continued to add that racial tensions in the country are as high as they'd ever been, and that his belief that President Obama would be a great cheerleader for the country didn't happen. Trump thinks he'd be a great cheerleader. "There's a lack of spirit," he said to the Washington Post's editorial board. "Because of this, a lot of people feel it's a hopeless situation."

He proposed incentives and economic zones for companies to move back into the inner cities and mentioned time and again the low spirit of the working class, especially prevalent in the African American community which feels left behind in the global conversation. The way Trump sees it, his proposition of a non-interventionist foreign policy will allow his administration – and indeed his supporters – to rebuild America, and make the country great again.

His proposition of cheerleading and morale boosting seems to undermine his initial rhetoric and tone as he campaigned all over the country. Like a trained performer, Trump managed to whip his audiences into a frenzy as he discussed some of his grander schemes, like his plans for the Southern Wall and his calls to deport millions of undocumented workers.

As things stand, Trump's incendiary, coded racial language hasn't done much to bring about a boosting of spirit among minority groups in the country. And when questioned about the sour relationship between the police and people of color in some areas he mostly deferred to his to support of law enforcement instead of digging in with a definitive answer.

"We are going to rebuild our infrastructure, which will become, by the way, second to none." In his acceptance speech Trump briefly touched on his campaign promise to rebuild his crumbling nation, and while infrastructure is a major issue for our government, there are no immediate financial means to meet the trillion-or-so dollars needed to rebuild our roads, bridges, airports, tunnels, hospitals, schools, etc.

His promise of rebuilding America's infrastructure is based on his economic incentives for the private sector. We're yet to find out whether corporations will take him up on his tax credits and similar enticements in exchange for their financial input. Trump's plan for America is ambitious compared to what Hillary Clinton offered her supporters, but the large funding gap that would undoubtedly remain as his plans are implemented is yet to be discussed.

A report was released by the American Society of Civil Engineers back in 2013, stating that the estimated investment required to restore the roads, bridges, and tunnels that Trump was talking about in his speech was about $3.4-trillion by 2020. In the same report the ASCE also described the condition of some of that infrastructure as dangerous, and with the potential to create havoc for major cities and towns across America unless addressed soon.

Capital investment in the country has dwindled over the past 50-years. One analysis done on California by the ASCE found that the state spent 20 cents of all tax dollars on infrastructure back in the 1950s and 1960s; and this had dropped to just 5 cents by the 1980s.

It's a genuine concern for the government and one that Trump plans to tackle by allocating large sums of money towards restorative infrastructure projects. The problem is that no one likes to think about infrastructure. People take it for granted until a disaster occurs and gets people's attention, forcing them to focus on things that should never have been ignored – much less ignored for decades.

Seeing the bigger picture

Forgotten infrastructure and loss of jobs have had a more profound impact on Latino and African American communities, although Donald Trump's borderline racist stance on immigration and crime led political commentators and other experts to declare massive Republican losses in these communities. But this election was far from normal and scientists were proven to have been wrong every step of the way. When members of the professional class make efforts to understand America's working-class and minority groups, they consult experts, who claim that the Trump movement gathered such a momentum mainly because of bigotry.

Large segments of the Democratic campaign attribute much of Trump's success to a bigoted, less educated white majority, but there's more to it than that. Case in point:

Debbie Biro, 57, from Nazareth, PA, is a churchgoing mother and lifelong Democrat – and also a yoga enthusiast who doesn't eat meat – experienced a dynamic political shift back in January when Trump skipped a debate in Iowa in order to host a fundraiser for veterans, something Biro said resonated with her. Her dad had served in the Korean War, and she thought it was nice that he was looking after the vets. She also admired his leadership, business skills, and believed he could get things done.

Tuesday's election showed scores of similar voters who are neither staunch conservatives nor supporters of Trump's alleged racist solutions to immigration and the economy. Also important to note are the numbers showing how a significant number of Latino and African American communities also voted for Trump.

53% of all white female voters supported Trump, according to exit polls, and they played a major role in his victory. Many of these women genuinely believe that America in on the wrong track, and that Trump alone can bring change.

Sure, they were incensed by allegations of sexual misconduct and the shocking recording of lewd sexual comments; but did any of these factors change their minds about the country, the economy, or American's foreign policy? No, and that's why they voted for Trump.

To many, it's a matter of perspective. Take the case of Biro; while female opponents went to Twitter branding Trump as a bloated misogynist and worse, she saw a "good man and a good father," and while other detractors said Trump had gone bankrupt and accused him of dodging taxes, his female supporters said they saw a man who built a successful real estate empire, proudly raised and promoted a beautiful daughter, and allowed a smart Washington female strategist to manage his campaign.

So in effect, they accepted Trump's sales pitch for himself.

To say that Trump supporters are "uneducated white men" is to misrepresent the people who put him into office. The fact that he said rude things about women did not escape his female supporters, but it didn't measure up to the other issues faced by Americans – and the world – today. It's not difficult to see their argument: "Trump has a beautiful family, and he wants to live in a beautiful country – the same country he was raised in. He wants the best for his kids and the only way to make that happen is by becoming president."

For the women who supported Trump, the economy was among their immediate concerns. They were also uneasy about immigration and the global threat of terrorism. Trump's message of building a wall did not deter the Latina vote to a large extent, as exit polls show that 26% of Latina women voted for him.

Research has long shown that both Democratic and Republican parties are open to having a female president. For some of the women who voted for Trump, any discussions about the campaign and their support for Trump tended to damage sisterly bonds, as many female Democratic voters mentioned Trump's controversies as a major deterrent.

According to one Democratic pollster, the entire party expected a national "surge of women" to support Hillary Clinton, but that did not happen. Although she managed to get a significant number of women in every demographic, Trump's victory was solid across the board.

Making America come first

If you watched his rally speeches at length, Trump seemed to ramble and boast and threaten like no other serious presidential aspirant has done in recent times. Some of his statements are clearly meant to enrage the establishment and fire up segments of his support base; but aside from that, his message is entirely legitimate.

In many of his rallies Trump spoke about trade. In fact, if we were to judge by how much time he spent discussing trade issues, it might be his biggest concern going into the White House – not white supremacy.

Of the issues most discussed by Trump, trade seems to be his obsession, especially regarding the free-trade deals that America has supported for decades and the

American companies that take their business abroad for economic reasons. He even talked about making phone calls to CEOs who have taken business elsewhere and threatening them with huge tariffs unless they come back to the U.S.

Another left-wing idea that Trump talked about more than once was competitive bidding in the drug industry. Apparently the U.S. doesn't competitively bid; something that shocks and horrifies the now-Republican president-elect (and this is another one of those interesting boondoggles of the Bush administration).

He also extended critique to the U.S. military industrial complex, which he says is often compelled to spend large amounts of money to purchase useless airplanes due to the power of industry lobbyists.

Trump had a curious selling proposition in his campaign: because I'm so rich and smart, my vast business empire hasn't been affected much by Washington's decisions to impose "bad" trade deals and support duplicitous business lobbyists and donations. And because I am free of the powerful, corrupting nature of modern campaign finance, I am best suited to make deals that are "good" for the citizens.

The issue of trade has polarized Americans by socio-economic status. To the ruling class and professional elites, who include most media executives and economists and Washington officials, the idea of "free trade" is something positive and noble that doesn't need probing into. But to the remaining 90% of Americans, trade doesn't mean the same thing. Consider the workers in a small rural plant who one morning discover that HQ has decided the company should move to Mexico, or some other location, for economic reasons. This requirement to "stay competitive" in what company executives call a "price-sensitive market" is just one of the reasons why businesses are closing and moving away, leaving thousands of Americans to struggle.

A map of Trump support coordinates very well with de-industrialization and despair, with all those areas that suffered economic drops thanks to Washington's free-market agreement that took businesses away voting for Trump. While it's true that some of his supporters hail from the old supremacist ideals, many more are simply excited at the prospect of having a new president that actually means what he says and who is going to bring the hammer down on the CEOs that fired so many people and brought poverty to America, unlike Barack Obama and Hillary Clinton. This is evidenced by recorded conversations with many of his white-majority supporters who, when asked about their leading concerns going into a new administration, all talk about the economy and their place in it. Support for Trump ran high among these people, including self-identified Democrats, but not because they are interested in witnessing a historic return of white supremacy. Instead, they want America to have more opportunities for them, and for their children to have "good jobs."

The reality is that Americans are far more frightened about the economy and state of world affairs to have overbearing bigoted feelings. Many recent studies confirm that people are tired and hurting because of the last several administrations' focus on other issues, including war and world dominance. The fact that Trump promises to bring the focus back onto America gives people hope that they haven't experienced in a while, perhaps since Reagan ran for office. Even the question of party identity comes secondary to the real issues affecting families across the country.

The election aftermath

The left-wing party in the U.S. stopped representing the common man a long time ago, choosing instead to morph into a tribune of the enlightened "creative class", a professional class that comes up with clever things like derivative securities and smartphone apps. Their efforts to further the goals of working people have long been forgotten, and as the ruling Democrats sat down to plan a strategic campaign, they figured these people had nowhere else to go.

What this election tells us is that these things should have been obvious to anybody who has set foot outside the rich enclaves of our two coasts. As Trump put it, "We've rebuilt China, and yet our country is falling apart. Our infrastructure… is like, Third-World." His words very clearly articulate a populist backlash that has been brewing for decades, with the elections being best way for the average person to vent their anger.

And yet many liberals cannot bring themselves to accept some of the blame for a growing frustration among the working-class, even for their blighted cities and diminishing income. It was far easier to scold them for expressing racist sentiment, and to close one's eyes to the painful reality that Trumpism isn't a silly campaign crusade and that in this day and age, neoliberalism has failed.

In the hours following Trump's victory, Twitter was alight with hashtags of people expressing shock, anger and confusion. But the presidency is not a personal decoration or accouterment that the citizens don at their pleasure, based on how it suits their prejudices and beliefs. Public office isn't a mood ring, either.

To undermine Trump's presidency with blatant rebellion is to be in denial. It's also undemocratic – un-American.

The potential of a Trump presidency

Republicans haven't had full control of the House, Senate, and Presidency at the same time since 1929. Republicans briefly controlled them for about two years under Eisenhower and George W. Bush, but by comparison, Democratic presidents have had control over Congress almost for their entire terms in office. This time, however, Republicans have a majority in the House and Senate and control a good number of state legislatures. Congress could pass new laws if Trump plays ball and actually agrees to sign them.

However this plays out, Middle America will want to see real change in the way things are done, being tired of the constant discourse from progressive community organizers, the media and Democrats. Mid-America is preparing to make a mark both socially and politically, and they've chosen Trump as their instrument of change.

RESULTS

2016	Winner	Loser
Nominee	Donald Trump	Hillary Clinton
Party	Republican	Democratic
Home State	New York	New York
Electoral Votes	306	232
States Won	30	20
Percentage of Votes Won	46.1%	48.0%
Number of Votes	62,686,675	65,240,114

*As of December 3, 2016.

REFERENCES

Bacon, Perry Jr. (July 22, 2015). How the Media Is Fueling Donald Trump's Campaign. Online: NBC News. Retrieved from http://www.nbcnews.com/politics/2016-election/how-media-fueling-donald-trumps-campaign-n395821.

Borosage, Robert L. (November 9, 2016). Why Trump Won. Online: The Nation. Retrieved from https://www.thenation.com/article/why-trump-won/.

Camosy, Charles. (November 9, 2016). Trump won because college-educated Americans are out of touch. Online: The Washington Post. Retrieved from https://www.washingtonpost.com/posteverything/wp/2016/11/09/trump-won-because-college-educated-americans-are-out-of-touch/?utm_term=.16a2aff7c890.

Donald Trump on Foreign Policy. (n.d.). Online: On the Issues. Retrieved from http://www.ontheissues.org/2016/Donald_Trump_Foreign_Policy.htm.

Fisher, Max. (November 11, 2016). What Is Donald Trump's Foreign Policy? Online: The New York Times. Retrieved from http://www.nytimes.com/2016/11/12/world/what-is-donald-trumps-foreign-policy.html.

Flegenheimer, Matt & Barbaro, Michael. (November 9, 2016). Donald Trump Is Elected President in Stunning Repudiation of the Establishment. Online: The New York Times. Retrieved from http://www.nytimes.com/2016/11/09/us/politics/hillary-clinton-donald-trump-president.html.

Frank, Thomas. (March 7, 2016). Millions of ordinary Americans support Donald Trump. Here's why. Online: The Guardian. Retrieved from

https://www.theguardian.com/commentisfree/2016/mar/07/
donald-trump-why-americans-support.

Graham, David A. (November 22, 2016). The Many Scandals of
Donald Trump: A Cheat Sheet. Online: The Atlantic.
Retrieved from
http://www.theatlantic.com/politics/archive/2016/11/donald
-trump-scandals/474726/.

Henderson, Barney. (October 8, 2016). Will the Donald Trump
lewd video controversy finally derail his presidential
campaign? Online: The Telegraph. Retrieved from
http://www.telegraph.co.uk/news/2016/10/08/will-the-
donald-trump-lewd-video-controversy-finally-derail-his/.

Kelly, A. & Sprunt, B. (November 9, 2016). Trump's First 100
Days: Here Is What The President-Elect Wants To Do.
Online: NPR. Retrieved from
http://www.npr.org/2016/11/09/501451368/here-is-what-
donald-trump-wants-to-do-in-his-first-100-days.

Lambert, Brian.(October 17, 2016). Post-election, the media will
have to examine its own role in the 2016 presidential
campaign. Online: MinnPost. Retrieved from
https://www.minnpost.com/media/2016/10/post-election-
media-will-have-examine-its-own-role-2016-presidential-
campaign.

Lee, Tremayne. (March 22, 2016). Donald Trump's plan to solve
the racial divide. Online: MSNBC. Retrieved from
http://www.msnbc.com/msnbc/donald-trumps-plan-solve-
the-racial-divide.

Mason, Gary. (November 11, 2016). Can Trump's plan restore
America's crumbling infrastructure? Online: The Globe
and Mail. Retrieved from
http://www.theglobeandmail.com/news/world/us-
election/can-trumps-plan-restore-americas-crumbling-
infrastructure/article32830057/.O'Connor, Lydia. (June 17,

2015). The DNC Has The Best Reaction To Donald Trump Announcing His Presidential Run. Online: The Huffington Post. Retrieved from http://www.huffingtonpost.com/2015/06/16/dnc-reaction-donald-trump_n_7596314.html.

Pilkington, Ed & Gabbatt, Adam. (November 9, 2016). How Donald Trump swept to an unreal, surreal presidential election win. Online: The Guardian. Retrieved from https://www.theguardian.com/us-news/2016/nov/09/how-trump-won-us-election.

Rosoff, Matt. (November 9, 2016). Why Trump won. Online: Business Insider. Retrieved from http://www.businessinsider.com/why-trump-won-2016-11.

Santucci, John & Stracqualursi. (June 16, 2015). Donald Trump Announces 2016 Presidential Campaign: 'We Are Going Make our Country Great Again'. Online: ABC News. Retrieved from http://abcnews.go.com/Politics/donald-trump-announces-2016-presidential-campaign-make-country/story?id=31799741.

Shalby, Colleen. (October 9, 2016). A brief history of the Trump campaign's controversies with women. Online: LA Times. Retrieved from http://www.latimes.com/politics/la-na-pol-trump-campaign-insults-women-20161009-snap-htmlstory.html.

Stephenson, E. & Kahn, C. (October 21, 2016). Trump gains on Clinton, poll shows 'rigged' message resonates. Online: Reuters. Retrieved from http://www.reuters.com/article/us-usa-election-idUSKCN12L1UI.

Stolberg, Sheryl Gay. (November 11, 2016). Why 53 per cent of America's white females voted for Donald Trump, even if they were offended by him. Online: National Post. Retrieved from http://news.nationalpost.com/news/world/why-53-per-cent-of-americas-white-females-voted-for-donald-trump-even-if-they-were-offended-by-him.

Tankersley, Jim. (November 9, 2016). How Trump won: The revenge of working-class whites. Online: The Washington Post. Retrieved from http://abcnews.go.com/Politics/donald-trump-announces-2016-presidential-campaign-make-country/story?id=31799741.

Zurcher, Anthony. (November 9, 2016). US Election 2016 Results: Five reasons Donald Trump won. Online: BBC News. Retrieved from http://www.bbc.com/news/election-us-2016-37918303.

1800

CHAPTER 2: The Revolution
THOMAS JEFFERSON VS. JOHN ADAMS

Thomas Jefferson   *John Adams*

---

[4] By Rembrandt Peale - White House Historical Association, Public Domain, https://commons.wikimedia.org/w/index.php?curid=1604678
[5] By Asher Brown Durand - This Image was released by the United States Navy with the ID 031029-N-6236G-001 (next).

The 4th United States quadrennial presidential election was held from the 31st of October until the 3rd of December 1800. Democratic-Republican Thomas Jefferson won the election with 61.4% of the vote earning 73 electoral votes and winning 9 states. His main challenger was Federalist Candidate John Adams.

The election of 1800 was the second election in which political parties were involved. The candidates for the Federalist party were incumbent President John Adams, who had been elected in 1796, and Charles Pinckney. For the Democratic-Republicans, it was Vice-president Thomas Jefferson and Aaron Burr.

The Setting

The political climate was fierce. Many of the ill sentiments stirred up in the 1796 election between the Federalists and the Democratic-Republicans continued and intensified over that four-year period prior to 1800. National and world events during that same time period also added to the differences between the parties. In what became a rematch of 1796, the so-called 'Revolution of 1800' brought forth many of the norms that are now part of party politics within a two-party system.

John Adams and the Federalists were identified as being pro-British and pro-centralized government. Thomas Jefferson and the Democratic-Republicans were seen as staunch opponents of centralized government and as being pro-French. Specific events, such as the Alien and Sedition Acts of 1798 fueled the Democratic-Republican's fears and rhetoric against the Federalists. They viewed those laws as being unconstitutional and being used to hinder the free speech of pro-Democratic-Republican newspaper editors and the advancement of Democratic-Republican values in general. The Federalists defended them as necessary to safeguard national security during the quasi-war that took place from 1798 to 1800 against France. This aggression against France was a direct consequence of the Jay Treaty and the toppling of the French monarchy by the French Revolution.

Even though the 1800 election, as the 1796 election immediately before it, was extremely polarized along what today would be called party-lines, the party system itself was still in an embryonic state. Factions existed within each party. Most notably within the Federalist party where Alexander Hamilton worked diligently behind the scenes against John Adams, encouraging support for the second Federalist candidate, Charles Pinckney.

Another factor that had a huge role in the 1800 election was the U.S. Constitution itself. Prior to the passing of the Twelfth Amendment, each elector in the electoral college would cast two votes for president. The candidate earning the most votes being elected president and the runner-up vice-president. This came into play in a big way in the election.

General Mood of Distrust

With the U.S. Constitution having been in effect for only eleven years, a national identity among the population had yet to develop. Even within the political parties themselves, national unity along party lines did not exist. The northern states distrusted the southern states and each political party distrusted the other. Loyalty and identification for citizens, as well as parties, was placed at a more local level -- the states. Every time that there was a national crisis the politicians, the fledgling press, and the citizenry were filled with talk and fears of disunion among the states. The concept that the United States was meant to be a permanent entity had yet to be properly forged.

Personal Attacks

During the 1796 election, Thomas Jefferson was accused of being at best a deist, and at worst an atheist with regards to his religious views. These attacks on Jefferson were reanimated during the 1800 election. Federalist supporters, using the accepted social paradigm of their age, used race as a way to attack Jefferson. False rumors were circulated intimating that Jefferson was part Native American or that his father had been half African American. Accusations of cowardice and weakness were hurled at Jefferson. These were loosely based on events from 1781 when Jefferson was governor of Virginia. At that time, as British troops were about to invade Richmond, the state capital, Jefferson and other key figures had evacuated the city.

The Democratic-Republicans lobbed insults at Adams, claiming that he was of "hermaphroditical character." Rumors were spread of Adams that he was loyal to the British Crown. He was labeled as being a hypocrite and tyrannical by journalists favoring the Democratic-Republican cause.

Even former First Ladies were not immune from being brought into the fray of this negative campaigning. Martha Washington's comment that Jefferson was "one of the most detestable of mankind" was widely circulated in pro-Adams campaign propaganda.

Political Machines Ahead of Their Time

The two principal candidates for each party, Adams and Jefferson, maintained the norm of the time by not actively campaigning themselves, depending instead on their surrogates to use innovative ways of getting their message out to the public.

Aaron Burr, the second Democratic-Republican candidate, established what would today be called a fully operational campaign headquarters in New York City. Based out of his home, Burr collected the names of every voter in the city. This list identified the financial condition, political leanings and temperament of each voter. Burr then had a team of volunteers and staff campaign door-to-door.

Thomas Jefferson retained the services of what today would be called a "political hatchet man," someone who manages the negative campaigning efforts. James Callender, a political satirist and pamphleteer, was retained to write a political pamphlet entitled, The Prospect Before Us. This was extremely critical of Adams and his administration. It introduced the narrative that Adams was fiercely pro-British and eager to attack France. It also intimated that Adams was corrupt, ignorant and desirous of establishing an aristocratic form of government.

For that pamphlet, Callender was prosecuted under the Sedition Act, found guilty and incarcerated. He was released on the last day of the Adams' administration.

The Outcome

The way that the Constitution was written meant

that each elector in the electoral college had two votes for president. There was no vote cast specifically for vice-president. The electors gave both the Democratic-Republican candidates, Jefferson and Burr, 73 votes each. Such a tie meant that the House of Representatives would have to determine who the next president would be.

Aaron Burr nearly became President over Jefferson.

It took 36 ballots before the House finally elected Thomas Jefferson as president. This was after strong pressure was applied by Federalist Alexander Hamilton

---

[6] Public Domain,
https://commons.wikimedia.org/w/index.php?curid=512714

on Federalist congressmen to support Jefferson over Burr. The argument used by Hamilton was that Jefferson "was not so dangerous a man" compared to Burr. Hamilton characterized Jefferson as having the wrong set of principles, but that Burr lacked them all together.

To the end, the election of 1800 was fierce, filled with bitterness and personal insult. However, it did mark the first transition of power from one party to another and it did so peacefully, in spite of all of the harsh politicking.

RESULTS

1800	Winner	Loser
Nominee	Thomas Jefferson	John Adams
Party	Democratic-Republican	Federalist
Home State	Virginia	Massachusetts
Electoral Votes	73	65
States Won	9	7
Percentage of Votes Won	61.4%	38.6%
Number of Votes	41,330	25,952

REFERENCES

Freeman, J. B. (n.d.) The Presidential Election of 1800: A Story of Crisis, Controversy, and Change. Online: The Gilder Lehrman Institute of American History. Retrieved May 19, 2016 from http://www.gilderlehrman.org/history-by-era/early-republic/essays/presidential-election-1800-story-crisis-controversy-and-change

Thomas Jefferson: Campaigns and Elections. (n.d.) Online: Miller Center of Public Affairs, University of Virginia. Retrieved May 19, 2016. http://millercenter.org-/president/biography/jefferson-campaigns-and-elections.

Ungar, R. (August 20, 2012). The Dirtiest Presidential Campaign Ever? Not Even Close! Online: Forbes Magazine. Retrieved May 19, 2016 from http://www.forbes.com/sites/rickungar/2012/08/20/the-dirtiest-presidential-campaign-ever-not-even-close/#3248fed83fea

Ferline, J. (November 1, 2004). Thomas Jefferson, Aaron Burr and the Election of 1800. Online: Smithsonian Magazine. Retrieved May 19, 2016 from http://www.smithsonianmag.com/history/thomas-jefferson-aaron-burr-and-the-election-of-1800-131082359/?no-ist

1828

CHAPTER 3: The Re-Match

ANDREW JACKSON VS. JOHN QUINCY ADAMS

7

8

Andrew Jackson   *John Quincy Adams*

---

[7] By Thomas Sully -
http://www.senate.gov/artandhistory/art/resources/graphic/xlarge/32_00018.jpg
[8] By George P. A. Healy - https://www.repro-tableaux.com/a/healy-george-peter-alexan/portrait-of-john-quincy-a.html

The 11th United States quadrennial presidential election was held from the 31st of October until the 2nd of December 1828. Democrat Andrew Jackson won the election with 56.0% of the vote earning 178 electoral votes and winning 15 states. His main challenger was National Republican Candidate John Quincy Adams.

The Jackson vs. John Quincy Adams election campaign of 1828 was marked by dirty tactics and brutality, and was considered by some as the very epitome of negative political campaigns in U.S. history.

In particular, this election was significant in the sense that it marked the election of a statesman who had previously been viewed as a true man of the people. However, the campaigning that year was notable on account of the intense personal attacks employed by supporters from both sides.

The challenger, Andrew Jackson, and the incumbent, John Quincy Adams, were starkly different. The only thing they, perhaps, had in common was their long careers in public service – one military, the other diplomatic.

By election time, both candidates had wild stories circulating about their pasts – with lurid charges of procuring of women, adultery, and murder. These stories were plastered on the pages of major partisan newspapers.

Background to the 1828 Election

Jackson and Adams had previously faced each other in the 1824 election, in what came to be referred to as "The Corrupt Bargain". So difficult was this race that the House of Representatives had to decide on the winner. At the time, Henry Clay, the Speaker of the House, had used his influence to ensure Adams won.

However, this did not deter Jackson. His fervent campaign against Adams resumed in 1825 immediately after Adams assumed the highest office in the land. Jackson, referred to as Old Hickory, and his supporters worked tirelessly to garner national support.

Although his power lay among rural voters and in the south, Jackson was still able to align himself with Martin Van Buren, a New York political broker. With

Van Buren's advisement, Jackson started appealing to northern working folk.

Party Conflict in 1828

In 1827, both Jackson and Adams' camps began in earnest with concerted efforts to besmirch the characters of their opponents. Although the candidates differed greatly on several substantial issues, the entire political campaign eventually found itself in the gutters. At the end of the day, the campaigns ended up being based on outrageously underhanded tactics.

The 1824 elections had not been affected by party affiliation. However, when Adams was in office, the defenders of the status quo started referring to themselves as National Republicans, while their opponents adopted the Democratic-Republicans (later shortened to Democrats) moniker.

As such, the election of 1828 introduced the U.S. to the two-party system, a precursor to modern politics. Martin Van Buren took up the role of organizing

Jackson's Democratic loyalists on account of his sharp political skills.

The negative political campaigns took several forms, including but not limited to personal attacks, accusation of adultery and other tactics designed to incent the voters.

Career Attacks

Knowing that Andrew Jackson had led a controversial life filled with violence and that he was famed for his abrupt and incendiary temper, those who detested him had a wealth of material to use. For example, Jackson had participated in a number of duels, killing one opponent in 1806. Similarly, in 1815 when Jackson was a troop commander, he had ordered the express execution of members of the militia who had been accused of desertion.

On the other hand, the Jackson camp mocked John Quincy Adams for his elitist stance. As a result, Adams' intelligence and refinement were turned against him. He was also derided as a Yankee at a time when this term was used to refer to shopkeepers known for taking advantage of their customers.

Adultery Rumors and Coffin Handbills

Despite the negative aspects of his career, Andrew Jackson was also considered a national hero on account of his military career and his winning of the Battle of New Orleans, which ended the War of 1812. John Binns, a Philadelphia printer, turned Jackson's military career and glory against him by publishing the notorious coffin handbill. This poster depicted 6 black coffins containing the bodies of the militiamen Jackson executed. It asserted that the militiamen had been murdered.

Similarly, questions surrounding Jackson's marriage started spreading across the county. His wife, Rachel had previously been married to another man. The questions, therefore, revolved around when she had started living with Jackson and the date of her divorce.

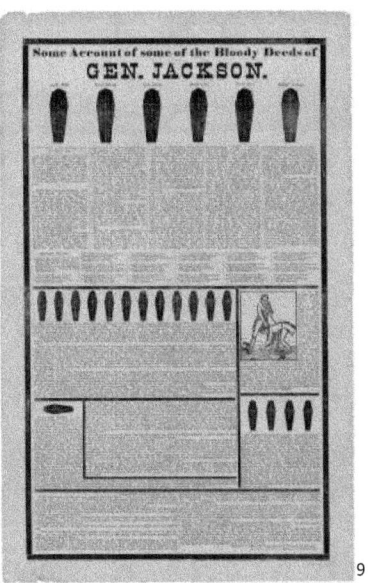

'Account of some of the Bloody Deeds of General Jackson.'

The Jackson camp explained that Jackson and Rachel believed she was divorced before they got married. However, there was and still is some doubt about the timing of these marital proceedings.

Attacks on John Q. Adams

John Quincy Adams, son of John Adams (second president and a founding father of the United States) began his career as the secretary to the American envoy

---

[9] By Unknown - Darlington Digital Library, University of Pittsburgh, Public Domain, https://commons.wikimedia.org/w/index.php?curid=44430090

to Russia during his teens. Thereafter, he developed into an illustrious career diplomatic and public servant. Later, this career formed the basis for his career in politics.

The Jackson team, therefore, began spreading rumors about Adams. In particular, they stated that while he served as the American ambassador to Russia, Adams had procured an American girl to provide sexual services to the reigning Russian Tsar.

Although the attack was baseless, the Jackson camp reveled in the rumors – even going as far as referring to Adams as a pimp and claiming that he was successful as a diplomat on account of his ability to procure women.

Adams was also attacked for maintaining a billiard table within the White House and charging the government for it. Although it is true that Adams enjoyed playing billiards in the White House, he paid for it using his personal funds.

The Culmination of the 1828 Rematch

When these scurrilous charges were revealed by partisan newspapers, Adams refused to get involved in further murk. So irked was he by the negative political campaigns, he refused to make notes in his diary from August until after the elections.

Jackson, however, was infuriated by the personal attacks on his person and his wife. He retaliated by becoming more involved in his own campaign. He even went so far as to write to newspaper editors providing them with guidelines to counter the attacks and encouraging them to launch their own attacks against Adams.

The Outcome

His appeal to the common folk eventually served him well. At the end of the election, he had won both the electoral vote and the popular vote. However, this victory came at a price – Rachel Jackson suffered cardiac arrest and died before his inauguration. Later, Jackson blamed his political enemies for the death.

As one of the worst of all negative political campaigns, the end was also besmirched by incredulous displays of ungentlemanly behavior. Jackson refused to pay the traditional courtesy call to Adams, and Adams refused to attend his opponent's inauguration. Indeed, the bitterness of the 1828 election resonated for years.

RESULTS

1828	Winner	Loser
Nominee	Andrew Jackson	John Quincy Adams
Party	Democratic	National Republican
Home State	Tennessee	Massachusetts
Electoral Votes	178	83
States Won	15	9
Percentage of Votes Won	56.0%	43.6%
Number of Votes	642,553	500,897

REFERENCES

Crane, D. (2009). Men of War. London: HarperPress.

Jackson, A. & Shaw, R. (1969). Andrew Jackson, 1767-1845. Dobbs Ferry, N.Y.: Oceana Publications.

Kamber, V. (1997). Poison Politics. New York: Insight Books, Plenum Press.

Parsons, L. (2009). The Birth of Modern Politics. Oxford: Oxford University Press.

Remini, R. (1963). The Election of Andrew Jackson. Philadelphia: Lippincott.

1864

CHAPTER 4: The Rail Splitter & the General

ABRAHAM LINCOLN VS. GEORGE MCCLELLAN

10   11

Abraham Lincoln   **George McClellan**

---

[10] By Alexander Gardner - http://www.britannica.com/bps/media-view/112498/1/0/0, Public Domain,
https://commons.wikimedia.org/w/index.php?curid=17639208
[11] By Matthew Brady - This media is available in the holdings of the National Archives and Records Administration.

The 20th United States quadrennial presidential election was held on 8th November 1864. Republican Abraham Lincoln won the election with 55.0% of the vote earning 212 electoral votes and winning 22 states. His main challenger was Democratic Candidate George McClellan.

Elections have always represented a period of great animosity and respect. However, modern day elections can be perceived to be more "civilized" compared to those of the past. One thing that remains constant irrespective of the times, elections are a time of great change and one election that represented a great change in the USA was the 1864 election between Abraham Lincoln and George McClellan. Historians find it particularly intriguing as it happened in the middle of the Civil War and it did end up shaping the future of the country.

The Republicans

For most people, Abraham Lincoln was a visionary, astute leader who championed the American philosophy of the 18th century. Unfortunately, many overestimate the popularity Lincoln had during his presidency. In the summer of 1864, Lincoln faced one of his biggest challenges - retaining his presidency. Before him, Andrew Jackson (1832) was the last president who had managed to serve for two terms. And, the country was in civil war. This war had ravaged the country as Union states fought the Confederate states. By 1864, they had been at war for nearly three years. Lincoln had lost hope of re-election and in writing on Aug 3, 1864, he conceded that "This morning, as for some days past, it seems exceedingly probable that this Administration will not be re-elected. Then it will be my duty to so co-operate with the President-elect as to save the Union between the election and the inauguration; as he will have secured his election on such ground that he cannot possibly save it afterward."[12] His political allies within the Republican Party had started to turn against him, and the Radical Republicans were backing General John C. Fremont as a third-party candidacy. He also did not get much love from the Democrats as both the "peace" wing

---

[12] Lincoln on Re-election. Source:
http://www.civilwar.org/education/history/primarysources/lincolns-letter-on-his.html?

and the "Copperheads" factions of the Democrats hated him. In addition, Lincoln had won the 1860 election without support from the South, which brought into question the strength of his presidency. In spite of the challenges Lincoln faced, in Baltimore on June 1864, Lincoln was nominated by the Republican Party to be their candidate for the presidency.

The Democrats

The Democratic Party was split into two factions, the "peace" wing and the "Copperheads". These two factions had different fundamental agendas and to move forward, they had to come up with a compromise. General George B. McClellan was nominated to be their candidate because he used to be in command of all Union armies. However, he had been removed from this position as Lincoln thought that he was too complacent in failing to attack the Southern Army often exaggerating the oppositions capabilities. The Democrats also decided to run on a peace platform. They had resolved that Lincoln's use of war as an attempt to unite the Union had failed, and that they wanted other more peaceful means to be adopted. They also wanted to maintain the Federal Union.

The War

By 1864, America had been at civil war for 3 years. Early on the Confederates seemed to have the advantage but at Gettysburg and Vicksburg General George Gordon Meade defeated Confederate General Robert E. Lee. In Gettysburg as an example, more than 170,000 American soldiers battled hard for three days, with over 50,000 casualties. The Confederates lost 28,000 of their men while the Union lost 23,000 men. This result was a bigger blow to the Confederates and it marked the beginning of the end for them. Despite these victories and what appeared to be a shift in momentum favoring the Union, Lincoln faced increasingly hateful opposition unlike any he had experienced before.

The Election

After both parties had nominated both its candidates, it was game on. While Lincoln initially had thought he would lose, events leading up to the election were showing fortune and favor towards him. As the race was tightening up, the 'Copperhead' and 'peace' platforms of Democratic Party were coming back to haunt them. A growing number of respected Democrats saw the party platforms as "treasonous" and would consequently fail to support the Democrats. This helped Lincoln win the military vote.

Lincoln's reelection fortunes further shifted when on July 22, 1864, Union Commander William T. Sherman led his forces in an attack on Atlanta, Georgia, burning down most of the city's buildings and structures including strategic military bases. This win was a considerable blow to the Confederates as their transportation infrastructure and hub was lost to them. He then marched down to Savannah on what is called "Sherman's march to the sea".

The victories in Georgia helped shift everything as news of the victory over the Confederates spread. Consequently, this led to Lincoln ordering for a day of thanksgiving and 100 gun salutes to the war heroes of Atlanta. Lincoln's popularity was now in full gear and he used his popularity to strike a blow to Fremont's 3rd party candidacy by getting rid of the conservative Postmaster-General Montgomery Blair. It worked as he won the support of the Radical Republicans.

Anti-McClellan campaign poster.

On November 8, 1864, elections were held, and Lincoln won with 55% of the votes compared to McClellan, who received 45% of the votes. Lincoln won the popular vote in 22 states along with 212 electoral votes while McClellan won only three states with a total

---

[13] By Thomas Nast, 1864. Sourced from http://www.sonofthesouth.net/Thomas_Nast.htm

of 21 electoral votes. The results were clear evidence of the political strength of Abraham Lincoln as he delivered a political knockout to the 'little' General.

The election was a nasty affair and it took great courage and political maneuvering for Lincoln to win. Although he was assassinated just 5 months after the election, his ability to see the war to a successful conclusion made Lincoln one of the most influential people in American history.

RESULTS

1864	Winner	Loser
Nominee	Abraham Lincoln	George McClellan
Party	National Union	Democratic
Home State	Illinois	New Jersey
Electoral Votes	212	21
States Won	22	3
Percentage of Votes Won	55.0%	45.0%
Number of Votes	2,218,388	1,812,807

REFERENCES

Democratic Party Platform. (n.d.). Online. Retrieved May 19, 2016, from http://www.sonofthesouth.net/union-generals/mcclellan/democratic-platform-1864.htm

The Importance of African-American Soldiers in Civil War History. (n.d.). Online. Retrieved May 19, 2016, from http://www.civilwar.org/resources/the-importance-of.html

The Election of 1864. (September 11, 2014). Online: Retrieved May 19, 2016 from http://www.ushistory.org/us/34e.asp

Achenbach, Joel. (n.d.). The election of 1864 and the last temptation of Abraham Lincoln. Online: Washington Post. Retrieved May 19, 2016 from https://www.washingtonpost.com/national/health-science/the-election-of-1864-and-the-last-temptation-of-abraham-lincoln/2014/09/11/e33f99aa-345b-11e4-9e92-0899b306bbea_story.html

Election of 1864 – Lincoln vs. McClellan. (n.d.). Online. Retrieved May 19, 2016 from www.campcurtin.org/pdfs/2014_3.pdf

Abraham Lincoln in Depth. (n.d.). Online. Retrieved May 19, 2016 from www.abrahamlincolnsclassroom.org

1872

CHAPTER 5: Satire and the Presidency

ULYSSES GRANT VS. HORACE GREELEY

14   15

Ulysses Grant   ***Horace Greeley***

---

[14] By Brady-Handy Photograph Collection (Library of Congress)
[15] By Unknown - Frederic Bancroft and William A. Dunning, A Sketch of Carl Schurz's Political Career, 1869-1906, facing p. 352.

The 22nd United States quadrennial presidential election was held on 5th November 1872. Republican Ulysses S. Grant won the election with 55.6% of the vote earning 286 electoral votes and winning 31 states. His main challenger was Democratic and Liberal Republican[16] Candidate Horace Greeley.

One of the most common and effective approaches to negative campaigning is mudslinging, a tactic where people run negative advertisements against their rivals. This method is aimed at discrediting the person's credibility, personality, stand, skills and opinions.

While an attack ad plainly exposes a rival's negative aspects, a contrasting ad uses positive aspects of the owner of the ad against negative aspects of the person's opponent. Just as the name suggests, it contrasts a contender's strengths to a rival's weaknesses.

The 1872 presidential election in the United States is perhaps the best historical confirmation of the negative effects of negative ad peddling. In this election, the

---

[16] Greeley was the candidate of BOTH the Liberal Republicans and Democrats.

incumbent was President Ulysses Grant, a Republican Party candidate who was seeking a second term.

During the campaigns, Cartoonist Thomas Nast, then working for Harper's Weekly, drew numerous satirical illustrations of Horace Greeley. Previously, the cartoonist's satirical yet controversial caricatures had helped in the ouster of a notorious New York City political strongman, Boss Tweed.

Afterwards, a number of politicians including congressional representatives, senators and even presidents sought the cartoonist's help against rivals. Thomas Nast was a staunch supporter of President Ulysses Grant. In fact, he detested anyone who opposed the president's policies, especially his role in winning the Civil War. Using his national fame, the cartoonist turned his talents on Greeley, the president's rival.

Precursor to the elections

Before entering politics, Horace Greeley was the editor and publisher of the famous New York Tribune, a competing publication of Harper's Weekly, Nast's employer.

After the Civil War, Horace Greeley had contributed money to bail out Jefferson Davis, then the former president of the Confederate States of America. This was just a few years before the election. The Confederacy included 11 southern states that had seceded from the United States shortly after the Presidential election of 1860 leading to the Civil War.

During the Civil War, more than 600,000 soldiers perished. This affected almost every American family in Northern and Southern states alike. Greeley sought to endear himself to the southerners and make reconciliations. In the process, he won the Democratic Party's nomination to run for presidency. However, Thomas Nast portrayed this as shaking bloody hands', since bitter memories still lingered from the Civil War that had ended just 7 years prior to the election.

Nast's cartoons of Greeley

The cartoonist found no trouble drawing cartoons of Greeley. His wispy beard, rumpled clothes, and wire glasses were outstanding aspects of the man in the cartoon. In one of the most famous caricatures, Thomas Greeley is depicted shaking hands with a murderer from the Confederate faction while stepping on a dead soldier from the Massachusetts 6th Regiment.

Cartoon of candidate Horace Greeley.

This and other cartoons depicting Horace Greeley in a negative light were famously circulated around the country. They communicated negative ideas about the incumbent's rival to mass audiences. This would lead to the defeat of Greeley by President Grant in the presidential elections.

When asked by friends about the impact of the cartoons, Greeley famously remarked, "I thought I was running for the presidency, not for the penitentiary."[17] The effects would actually land him in a place worse the penitentiary - his grave.

The death of Horace Greeley

Just three weeks after Election Day, Horace Greeley died. His death resulted in a split of his votes as electors in the Electoral College cast their votes for four different presidential candidates. Interestingly, the late Greeley received three electoral college votes posthumously. However, Congress disallowed these votes as the law barred voting for a deceased person. It was the first and the only presidential election in the United States that a leading candidate died during the election process.

Greeley's wife had actually died just a few days before the vote. Many schools of thought pointed at Nast's cartoons as playing a role in the death of the

---

[17] See http://coffeewithken.blogspot.com/2012/08/how-negative-can-campaign-get-thomas.html

politician and his wife. While some people congratulated Nast for assisting in the ouster of New York political strongman Boss Tweed, others ridiculed him for the defeat of Horace Greeley and their ensuing deaths.

Lessons from the election

Today, political and journalism students alike study the role of Thomas Nast in early American politics. Professors outline his outstanding talent in art as well as his excellence at political journalism.

The negative political campaigning from this election emphasizes the fact that a person can actually be elected president after a smear campaign on his closest rival whether directly or using proxies.

Apart from negative ad peddling, other smear campaigns that worked in this election include voter suppression, fear mongering and push poll tactics. Experts state that these approaches motivate a base for the owner of the campaign while alienating undecided voters from taking part. As voter turnout decreases, the political atmosphere is somewhat radicalized.

However, these campaigns do not always work for the candidate whose faction sponsors them. In some cases, the targeted candidate releases a stronger counterattack as a reply to the smear campaign, effectively causing a backlash from registered prospective voters.

RESULTS

1872	Winner	Loser
Nominee	Ulysses Grant	Horace Greeley
Party	Republican	Liberal Republican
Home State	Illinois	New York
Electoral Votes	286	3
States Won	31	6
Percentage of Votes Won	55.6%	43.8%
Number of Votes	3,598,235	2,834,761

REFERENCES

1872 Election Results Grant vs. Greeley. (n.d.). Retrieved May 19, 2016 from http://www.historycentral.com/elections/1872.html

Ackerman, Ken. (August 8, 2012). How negative can a campaign get? Thomas Nast's attacks on Horace Greeley, 1872. Online. Retrieved May 19, 2016 from http://coffeewithken.blogspot.co.ke/2012/08/how-negative-can-campaign-get-thomas.html

Luta, Alexandra. (n.d.). President Ulysses S. Grant: Election, Successes and Corruption. Online. Retrieved May 19, 2016 from http://study.com/academy/lesson/president-ulysses-s-grant-election-successes-and-corruption.html

1876

CHAPTER 6: The End of Reconstruction

RUTHERFORD HAYES VS. SAMUEL TILDEN

18   19

Rutherford Hayes   **Samuel Tilden**

---

[18] By Brady-Handy Photograph Collection (Library of Congress)
[19] By Unknown -
http://www.copyrightexpired.com/hawkins/nyc/bwh_sm_samuel_j_tilden.jpg

The 23rd United States quadrennial presidential election was held on 7th November 1876. Republican Rutherford B. Hayes won the election with 47.9% of the vote earning 185 electoral votes and winning 21 states. His main challenger was Democratic Candidate Samuel Tilden.

The 1876 election has been called the ugliest presidential campaign ever. Samuel Jones Tilden – who was the Democratic party candidate – was opposed by Rutherford B. Hayes, an attorney turned Republican party candidate from Delaware, Ohio. Despite the early returns that foreshadowed an easy Tilden victory, the election process turned into one of the ugliest mudslinging exercises ever. Hayes accused his opponent of taking bribes while simultaneously calling him a liar and even a "syphilitic drunk". At the same time, voter fraud became an everyday occurrence and the election went exactly where Hayes wanted it to go, providing some of the very first examples of a successful negative campaign.

The Outcome

The outcome of the election could not be decided in several states which turned out to be a key factor. As the election process stumbled on, the more chaotic the process of selecting the President became. At one point, Tilden with 184 electoral votes only needed one more to get the 185 he needed for the Presidency while Hayes had only 165. From the initial vote, it took months before a victor emerged but the legitimacy of the win forever remains tarnished. The whole thing almost led to another civil war but luckily, the election process ended before that could happen. The election was ended by a deal made behind closed doors, giving Hayes the presidency on the promise that he would pull troops out of the South.

On the Verge of Victory

On the night of November 7, 1876, Tilden thought he was going to be the president of the United States. He had the support and he had the votes (he possessed more than 51% of the votes at the time). His presence foreshadowed better times and prosperity to Democrats, who were often ignored by the political powers after the

Civil War. Tilden was a smart corporate lawyer who also knew what was needed to be done in order to win the election. Yet, in a twisted turn of events, it all went sideways because of a successful negative campaign. While Hayes ended up winning the election, one could argue that everybody lost. The mudslinging process was thorough and relentless.

Mudslinging Begins

As the post-election politicking heated up, Tilden's whole life was taken apart starting with his health and his role in the railroad industry, which was pretty much the emblem of corporate corruption at the time. Tilden was 62 and as someone who never had a wife, he was looked upon as somewhat of a boring person, but he was still respected in Democratic circles. His candidacy also could not have come at a seemingly better time, as the regime in power led by president Ulysses S. Grant found themselves facing serious corruption charges. Everything was set up for Tilden to save the whole Democratic party from imploding. He got the votes in many states but because Louisiana, Florida, and South Carolina were still undecided after the election, Hayes was given renewed life in his personal fight for the Presidency.

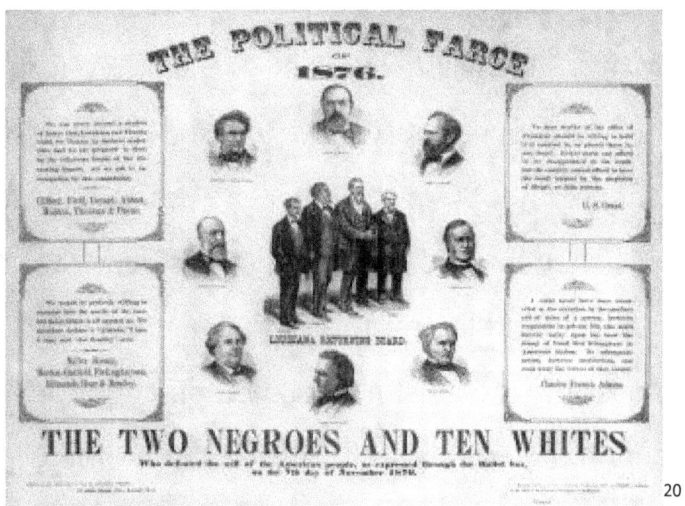

20

Poster about the 'stolen election'.

Several of Tilden's votes were disqualified without any apparent legitimate reason. Several states reported infractions and bribery attempts on both fronts. Associate Justice Joseph P. Bradley turned out to be the decisive vote, forever changing American political history. According to several sources, he was ready to cast his vote in favor of the Democratic party up until the last moments.

---

[20] By N.J. Newark - The Library of Congress Prints & Photographs Online Catalog; http://www.loc.gov/rr/print/catalog.html

Various Democratic representatives were present in his home on the eve of the election, leaving with the understanding that they had secured his vote. Little did they know that Senator Frederick T. Frelinghuysen and Secretary of the Navy, George M. Robeson would arrive for some late night lobbying. Together, they managed to convince Bradley that the Democratic Presidency would be a huge failure and their effort turned out to be the final and quite possibly the most important moment of the whole election process. With Bradley's "turn of fate" vote in their pocket, Rutherford B. Hayes managed to win the presidential electoral tally by exactly one vote (Bradley's), 185 to 184. The rest is history.

After Hayes was finally declared the winner, he pulled U.S. Troops out of the south. This action affectively ended reconstruction as the southern democrats once again were able to assert themselves which meant a partial return to the past. Many of the promised gains never materialized as voting rights, and many other rights were either taken away from blacks, or never delivered on. The effects of this election were felt for over 100 years and in some ways still linger on today.

RESULTS

1876	Winner	Loser
Nominee	Rutherford Hayes	Samuel Tilden
Party	Republican	Democratic
Home State	Ohio	New York
Electoral Votes	185	184
States Won	21	17
Percentage of Votes Won	47.9%	50.9%
Number of Votes	4,034,311	4,288,546

REFERENCES

The Disputed Presidential Election of 1876. (n.d.) Online: Digital History. Retrieved May 19, 2016 from http://www.digitalhistory.uh.edu/disp_textbook.cfm?smtID=2&psid=3109

Hayes-Tilden Election (1876). (n.d.) Online: PBS. http://www.pbs.org/wnet/jimcrow/stories_events_election.html

The Election of 1876 & The End of Reconstruction. (n.d.) Online: Authentic History. Retrieved May 19, 2016 from http://www.authentichistory.com/1865-1897/1-reconstruction/4-1876election/index.html

Election of 1876. (n.d.). Online: Laws. Retrieved May 19, 2016 from http://constitution.laws.com/election-of-1876

1888

CHAPTER 7: 'Ma, Ma Where's My Pa?'
GROVER CLEVELAND VS. JAMES BLAINE

21   22

Grover Cleveland   **_James Blaine_**

---

[21] United States Library of Congress
[22] By Mathew Brady – United States Library of Congress Prints and
Photographs Division. Brady-Handy Photograph Collection.

The 25th United States quadrennial presidential election was held on 4th November 1884. Democrat Grover Cleveland won the election with 48.9% of the vote earning 219 electoral votes and winning 20 states. His main challenger was Republican Candidate James Blaine.

While it is accepted now that television and in fact multi-media advertising has opened a whole new avenue for negative campaigning, that doesn't mean that campaigns were gentlemanly affairs prior to the advent of television advertisements.

The election of 1884 is famous for the new lows that the two presidential candidates – Grover Cleveland and James G. Blaine – found themselves sinking to. It was an election that was marred by accusations against Cleveland about fathering an illegitimate child, and allegations of corruption against Blaine.

This was an election that would set the stages for how elections were run, or not run. What is generally considered to be Blaine's biggest downfall as a presidential candidate are the supposed "Mulligan

Letters". Leading up the 1876 election, in which Blaine had been a heavy favorite, he found himself under fire for selling almost-worthless bonds to the Union Pacific Railroad for tens-of-thousands of dollars. This was seen as one step away from a bribe, although Blaine was adamant that this was not the case. He argued that it was a completely above-board stock and bonds transaction, and that he had conducted such business with the Union Pacific Railroad plenty before that.

Digging up dirt

During an investigation set forth by the House of Representatives, a man from Boston named James Mulligan, who had worked for Blaine's brother-in-law, claimed he had a set of letters sent between Blaine and Warren Fisher, a railroad lawyer who was also from Boston, proving that Blaine had set up the transaction as a bribe. The end of the letter stated: "Kindly burn this letter" [23].

While the investigation committee took a recess

---

[23] See
https://presidentialcampaignselectionsreference.wordpress.com/overviews/19th-century/1884-overvie/

from the hearings, it is believed that Blaine and Mulligan met in a hotel room and Blaine ended up in possession of the letters.

Blaine's correspondence with Fisher was damning, and it helped cost him the nomination in 1876. However, when most people had forgotten about the Mulligan Letters after Blaine secured the nomination in 1884, the Boston Journal accessed portions of the letters that had not yet seen the light of day, including the one with the now-infamous line "Burn this Letter".

It was because of Blaine's purported political corruption that many Republicans, now known as "Mugwumps"[24] flocked to the side of Grover Cleveland in 1884, unable to handle the thought that a man so obviously swayed by money would be the face of their party for at least four years, if not eight. And even in the Gilded Age, where corruption was rampant and accepted as the norm, it was not good to have someone so open to the public eye to be so obvious in their adherence to bribery and quid-pro-quo agreements.

---

[24] see presidentialcampaignselectionsreference.wordpress.com

Blaine's campaign ran into another painful problem – the reverend Samuel D. Burchard introduced Blaine at his church after stating, "We are Republicans, and don't propose to leave our party and identify ourselves with the party whose antecedents have been Rum, Romanism, and Rebellion,"[25]. This is widely reported to have helped alienate Blaine from New Yorkers and Southerners (who specialized in Romanism and Rebellion respectively). John St. John, a third party candidate who often helped sway voters over to the Republican side, campaigned vigorously in 1884 for the Democratic Party, effectively losing Blaine the state of New York. And in an election where the popular vote was decided by .2%[26], the electoral votes Cleveland gained and Blaine lost could have meant the election if the results had been reversed.

The Other Party

Cleveland's campaign was not without its own problems, however. As a bachelor it was often assumed

---

[25] see
http://history1800s.about.com/od/presidentialcampaigns/a/electionof1884.htm
[26] See http://www.historycentral.com/elections/1884.html

that he had at least one mistress during his short term as Governor. During the election, word broke out that he had fathered an illegitimate child with a woman named Maria Halpin. And because of it, one of the most infamous campaign chants was born. Republicans would chant at Cleveland, "Ma, Ma, Where's My Pa? (Gone to the White House, Ha Ha Ha!)"[27].

'Ma, Ma, where's my Pa?'

In a bizarre turn for national politics, Grover Cleveland elected to tell the truth. Maria Halpin was a woman who was known to have more than a few gentleman callers, including a man for whom the child was named. Cleveland, being the only eligible bachelor of the bunch, actually assumed responsibility for taking

---

[27] See http://reason.com/archives/2006/10/13/the-10-dirtiest-political-race
[28] By Frank Beard (1842–1905) - Library of Congress Print and Picture Collection [1]

care of the child, despite not quite knowing whether the child was his or another man's entirely. This won Cleveland an overwhelming amount of respect. He met a scandal that, for its time was huge (a scandal today discussing illegitimate children is still large – but back then, when a man Cleveland's age should have been married for decades by that point in his life, it was ground-breaking news). Cleveland knew that it was a scandal that could make or break his campaign, and he elected to meet it head on. In a fun twist of events, once Cleveland won the nomination and found himself in the White House, the cry of, "Ma, Ma Where's My Pa!" became a slogan for the Democratic Party, used to mock the Republicans who couldn't even beat a candidate with an (almost) confirmed illegitimate child.

The Outcome

Grover Cleveland won the election of 1884, in a year where the policy platforms and ideological standpoints of the candidates didn't matter as much as whether or not they were seen as decent people. While Blaine came off as elusive and corrupt, Cleveland came off as fallible and honest. Even though someone who makes the mistake of siring an illegitimate child may not seem like the worthiest candidate to hold the Oval Office (well, in the 19th century, at least), the fact that he was able to step outside of the political norm and "tell the truth" (as he told his campaign staff) was seen as a very valuable asset to have in a President. However, the silver lining is that while Blaine had much more go wrong for his campaign than went right, he only lost by 37 electoral votes – 36 of which belonged to New York.

The election of 1884 set the stage for other fierce campaigns in the mid-to-late 20th century, including Nixon-McGovern in 1972, Bush-Dukakis in 1988, and Bush-Clinton in 1992.

RESULTS

1884	Winner	Loser
Nominee	Grover Cleveland	James Blaine
Party	Democratic	Republican
Home State	New York	Maine
Electoral Votes	219	182
States Won	20	18
Percentage of Votes Won	48.9%	48.3%
Number of Votes	4,914,482	4,856,905

REFERENCES

Goodman, B. K. (n.d.). 1884 – Presidential Campaigns and Elections. Online. Retrieved May 11, 2016, from https://presidentialcampaignselectionsreference.wordpress.com/overviews/19th-century/1884-overvie/

The Election of 1884 Was Marked By Gaffes and a Looming Scandal. (2014, November 22). Online. Retrieved May 11, 2016, from https://history1800s.about.com/od/presidentialcampaigns/a/electionof1884.htm

1884 Presidential Elections. (n.d.). Online. Retrieved May 11, 2016, from http://www.historycentral.com/elections/1884.html

Mark, D. (2006, November). The 10 Dirtiest Political Races in U.S History. Online. Retrieved May 11, 2016, from http://reason.com/archives/2006/10/13/the-10-dirtiest-political-race

1964

CHAPTER 8: Landslide!

LYNDON JOHNSON VS. BARRY GOLDWATER

29

30

Lyndon Johnson   *Barry Goldwater*

---

[29] By Arnold Newman, White House Press Office (WHPO) -
http://photolab.lbjlib.utexas.edu/detail.asp?id=18170
[30] By Trikosko, Marion S., photographer -
http://www.loc.gov/pictures/item/2009632121

The 45th United States quadrennial presidential election was held on 3rd November 1964. Democrat Lyndon Johnson won the election with 61.1% of the vote earning 486 electoral votes and winning 44 states. His main challenger was Republican Candidate Barry Goldwater.

However, this victory came on the back of one of the nastiest presidential campaigns ever carried out. The Johnson campaign turned negative adverts into something of an art-form. They used negative ads so sleekly that the 1964 campaign is now considered the hallmark of negative campaigning.

Background

To fully understand why the ads were so successful, it is important to have a basic grasp of the state of the nation in 1964. The 1964 presidential campaigns occurred against the backdrop of the assassination of President John F. Kennedy ('JFK'). JFK was an extremely popular president who had been gunned down on November 22, 1963. At the time of his death, JFK was setting the stage for his reelection campaign. Following his death, the Democratic Party decided to support President Lyndon B. Johnson as their candidate.

The tragedy of JFK's assassination left the Republicans with a conundrum as they could not directly attack JFK's policies. This would make them appear insensitive to the memory of a beloved former president. They couldn't attack Johnson either, since many people saw him as JFK's natural successor. An attack on Johnson could easily be construed as an attack on JFK's legacy.

Johnson's campaign strategists perfectly understood the Republicans' predicament. They knew that they could fling mud at the Republicans – and the latter would feel awkward retaliating in kind. And that is exactly what they did.

However, the Republicans were actually complicit in the Democrats' use of negative campaigning. This is because their presidential candidate – Senator Barry Goldwater – provided the perfect target for negative campaigning.

The Perfect Target

Goldwater was an ultra-conservative Senator from Arizona. He was renowned for his frankness, outspokenness, and extreme views. Unfortunately, his thoughtless remarks often provided the perfect fodder for the Johnson campaign to attack him.

For instance, Goldwater once remarked that he would use nuclear weapons in situations which others found unacceptable. Being a strong supporter of the Vietnam War, he had suggested escalating the conflict – to the point of using nuclear weapons, if necessary – to ensure victory. He also once joked that the US military should "lob one [a nuclear weapon] into the men's room of the Kremlin"[31].

On another occasion, Goldwater was quoted saying: "Sometimes I think this country would be better off if we could just saw off the eastern seaboard and let it float out to sea."[32]

These extremist views formed the basis of the

[31] See https://campaignrhetoric.wordpress.com/?s=kremlin
[32] Ibid.

negative attacks on Goldwater. They offered the Johnson campaign with the perfect ammunition to paint Johnson as extremist, genocidal and up to no good. They did this through well-crafted ads.

The Negative Advertisements

The most famous ad released during the 1964 presidential elections was the "Daisy Girl" or "Peace, Little Girl". This ad – which is sometimes simply referred to as "Daisy" – is considered the most effective negative political ad of all time. To date, it is still considered a masterpiece of negative advertising – so much so that in 2014, numerous newspapers commemorated its 50th anniversary.

The Daisy Girl played on Johnson's apparent willingness to use nuclear weapons. It super-imposed a video of a little girl counting petals off a daisy, with a voice counting down a missile launch. At the climax, there was a nuclear explosion, followed by a message from Johnson: "To make a world in which all of God's children can live, or to go into the dark. We must either love each other, or we must die."

Image from the famous 'Daisy' advertisement.

The Daisy Girl is said to have been singly responsible for damaging Goldwater's presidential ambitions. It basically painted him as having the potential to start a nuclear war – a real fear in 1964. The ad actually aired only once, and was pulled out due to heavy criticism. Even then, the damage it did was irrevocable. It sparked debates which lasted throughout the campaign.

However, the Johnson campaign did not stop at the Daisy Girl. They released another ad called "Eastern Seaboard". This ad played on Goldwater's statement about the Eastern Seaboard (quoted above). This attack ad painted Goldwater as impulsive, unpatriotic and childish. It is was also extremely effective in eroding his credibility as president. In fact, if it wasn't for the Daisy Girl, Eastern Seaboard would have been considered the most effective presidential attack ad ever.

The Johnson campaign also released another ad called "KKK for Goldwater". This ad basically branded Goldwater as a racist. The basis of the ad was the fact that Robert Creel – the KKK leader in Alabama – had openly declared his support for Goldwater.

Barry fights back

The Goldwater campaign tried to fend off the accusations made in the various ads. For instance, the campaign accused Johnson of twisting Goldwater's words on nuclear weapons. Goldwater himself attempted to explain off his stance on nuclear weapons – claiming that his primary intention is to defend American interests. He also denied being a racist or having any KKK links and claimed that the Eastern Seaboard comment was a joke.

Even then, the adverts put Goldwater on the defensive. He spent most of the time responding to the scathing attacks, instead of articulating his policies. To further complicate matters, his campaign could not engage in negative attacks against Johnson. This is because the latter offered little ammunition, and attacking JFK wasn't an option. In the end, the negative campaigns took their toll, and Goldwater was trounced quite easily.

In a nutshell, the 1964 elections saw some of the fiercest negative campaigns ever carried out. The negative ads were mostly deployed against the Republican candidate, Barry Goldwater. However, it was Goldwater himself who provided the ammunition used against him. Lyndon B. Johnson's campaign strategists were more than happy to exploit Goldwater's outspokenness to their advantage. They ran one of the nastiest campaigns ever – and won by some margin.

RESULTS

1964	Winner	Loser
Nominee	Lyndon Johnson	Barry Goldwater
Party	Democratic	Republican
Home State	Texas	Arizona
Electoral Votes	486	52
States Won	44	6
Percentage of Votes Won	61.1%	38.5%
Number of Votes	43,127,041	27,175,754

REFERENCES

1964 Elections Johnson vs Goldwater. (n.d.) Online: History Central. Retrieved May 19, 2016 from http://www.historycentral.com/elections/1964.html

Walsh, K. T. (September 17, 2008). The Most Consequential Elections in History: Lyndon Johnson and the Election of 1964. Online: U.S. News & World Report. Retrieved May 19, 2016 from http://www.usnews.com/news/articles/2008/09/17/the-most-consequential-elections-in-history-lyndon-johnson-and-the-election-of-1964

Election 1964 – Johnson v Goldwater. (n.d.) Online: Eagleton Institute of Politics. Retrieved May 19, 2016 from http://www.eagleton.rutgers.edu/research/americanhistory/ap_1964.php

Levy, M. (n.d.) United States presidential election of 1964. Online: Encyclopaedia Britannica. Retrieved May 19, 2016 from http://www.britannica.com/event/United-States-presidential-election-of-1964

1972

CHAPTER 9: Watergate, War, and Scandal

RICHARD NIXON VS. GEORGE MCGOVERN

33   34

Richard Nixon   ***George McGovern***

---

[33] United States Library of Congress
[34] By Gary Yanker - This image is available from the United States Library of Congress's Prints and Photographs division under the digital ID yan.1a38272.

The 47th United States quadrennial presidential election was held on 7th November 1972. Republican Richard Nixon won the election with 60.7% of the vote earning 530 electoral votes and winning 49 states. His main challenger was Democratic Candidate George McGovern.

George McGovern won the Democratic Party nomination after running an antiwar campaign against Richard Nixon. McGovern, a senator from North Dakota who served in World War II as a member of the U.S Army Air Corps, took a strong position on various social issues such as the women's movement, and homosexuality. He strongly opposed United States' involvement in the Vietnam War. On the other hand, the incumbent president Richard Nixon was vice president in 1952 under Eisenhower and had also served as a lieutenant commander in the Navy. Emphasizing his success in foreign affairs and a good economy, Richard Nixon won the Presidential election in a landslide.

Nixon was first elected president in 1972 and in his first term, had accomplished a number of things including the ending of the military draft, establishing a broad environmental program, and creating new anticrime laws. And in his quest for world stability, Nixon had focused on reducing tension with the U.S.S.R and China. As a result, incumbent president Richard Nixon was nominated by the Republican Party for a second term in the 1972 U.S presidential election.

Background of the 1972 Presidential election

By 1971, President Richard Nixon's approval rate had fallen below 50 percent. Unemployment and inflation were rising. On the other hand, the Vietnam War was still dragging on despite the promises he had made in 1968. Nixon managed to restore his popularity through various actions; ending the draft, instituting price and wage controls, ordering the bombing of Hanoi in a bid to end the war, and taking unprecedented diplomatic trips to Russia and china.

Richard Nixon's opponent, Senator George McGovern, won the Democratic Party's nomination with a campaign that was sparked by the anti-war movement and a reduction in military spending. McGovern named fellow Senator, Thomas Eagleton from Missouri as his Vice Presidential running mate. However, shortly after the convention, Thomas Eagleton revealed that he had received shock therapy after being hospitalized for depression. Since the incident created an impression of ineptitude, Thomas Eagleton was dropped from the ticket and McGovern replaced him with R. Sargent Shriver, a former ambassador. Moreover, McGovern was unable to convince the general public of any possible connection between the Watergate incident and the Nixon administration.

Nixon and McGovern Ads

Both candidates in the 1972 election aired two different ads. George McGovern mainly focused on Richard Nixon's negative aspects in his campaign ads. The Watergate scandal stems from the June break-in at the Watergate Apartment Complex offices of the Democratic National Committee Headquarters. Although the break-in was traced back to the committee of the President's re-election, Richard Nixon denied any involvement.

One ad run by the McGovern Campaign pieced together numerous newspaper articles that depicted Nixon in a negative light. "Nixon's Ex-Aides and Five Others indicted in Bugging Case", "President's Credibility under Attack", and "FBI finds Nixon Aides Sabotaged Democrats". A voiceover had a man speaking telling the audience what Richard Nixon was really about; "This is all about the government, it's about bugging, it's about lying, it's about spying, and it's about credibility". He also says; "And, this is how you stop it; with your vote" with Richard McGovern's name in big bold letters across the screen.

Releasing a campaign commercial focusing on the Watergate scandal was a bold move on McGovern's side bearing in mind that the scandal was not fully public yet. McGovern chose to focus on the scandal instead of emphasizing what he was planning to do for the United States once he was elected.

Nixon on the other hand, chose a very different approach in his campaign ads. His showed him as a successful leader and George McGovern as a very reckless liberal. His campaign ran positive ads that focused on Nixon's achievements during his first term in office instead of putting George McGovern down. For instance, his commercials featured the "Nixon Now" song which is a happy and upbeat song. Additionally, his ads were filled with images that did not even have anything to do with Richard Nixon. They showed butterflies, people running through the rain, and people playing in water. Nixon used his ads to make people think and feel that things were better and that they were happier with him as president.

Nixon's positive ads also included posters of people expressing love for their president and a lot of pictures of Nixon shaking hands with many different people. Nixon did have numerous positive achievements as president. Therefore, focusing on his positive aspects and success rather than bringing down George McGovern's negative aspects was a good choice. It allowed the public to see his success as a way of proving to them that he was indeed a credible presidential candidate for re-election.

Nixon's most effective ads however, were attack ads. For example, one commercial ridiculed the defense cuts McGovern had proposed by using the image of a hand sweeping away planes, warships, and soldiers. Another ad claimed that George McGovern would put 47% of the population on welfare. The main purpose of this strategy was to create the impression that the liberal views of McGovern had put him outside the Democrats' mainstream.

In the general presidential election campaign, George McGovern called for withdrawal from the Vietnam War. He also proposed various liberal democratic policies which included guaranteed minimum income for the poor. However, his campaign was largely undermined when he restructured his primary process. Besides weakening his campaign, his disloyalty to Eagleton and the perception that the foreign policy he proposed was too extreme also alienated many democrats.

The Outcome

The 1972 presidential election resulted in Richard

Nixon's re-election in a landslide which was one of the biggest in American presidential election history. In fact, Massachusetts was the only state that George McGovern won. The use of both positive and negative ads showed how vital effective marketing is in persuading voters to vote or not to vote for certain candidates.

RESULTS

1972	Winner	Loser
Nominee	Richard Nixon	George McGovern
Party	Republican	Democratic
Home State	California	South Dakota
Electoral Votes	520	17
States Won	49	1
Percentage of Votes Won	60.7%	37.5%
Number of Votes	47,168,710	29,173,222

REFERENCES

1972 Presidential Election. (n.d.). Online. Retrieved May 19, 2016 from http://www.270towin.com/1972_Election/

1972 Elections McGovern vs. Nixon. (n.d.). R Online. etrieved May 19, 2016 from http://www.historycentral.com/elections/1972.html

Freidel, F. and Sidey, H. (2006). The Presidents of the United States of America. Online.: White House Historical Society. Retrieved May 19, 2016 from https://www.whitehouse.gov/1600/presidents/richardnixon

The Election of 1972. (n.d.). Online. Retrieved May 19, 2016 from https://www.boundless.com/u-s-history/textbooks/boundless-u-s-history-textbook/the-conservative-turn-of-america-1968-1989-30/the-nixon-administration-224/the-election-of-1972-1269-9282/

1988

CHAPTER 10: 7 Dwarves, Tanks, and Willie

GEORGE H.W. BUSH VS. MICHAEL DUKAKIS

35   36

George H.W. Bush   *Michael Dukakis*

---

[35] By Library of Congress
[36] By Photo taken by Hal O'Brien.

The 51st United States quadrennial presidential election was held on 8th November 1988. Republican George H. W. Bush won the election with 53.4% of the vote earning 426 electoral votes and winning 40 states. His main challenger was Democratic Candidate Michael Dukakis.

In 1952, Dwight Eisenhower was America's first politician to campaign using television. For many years since then, television advertising has been an effective tool for presidential hopefuls in the United States. Since voters have little physical contact with presidential contenders, candidates rely on the mass media to inform voters and attract supporters.

As the leader of a presidential campaign, any presidential candidate presumably has a significant amount control of the material that goes on air and onto people's screens. Many research studies have indicated that voters are swayed by television advertising. A TV ad influences people's perception of a candidate's personality while altering previously unfavorable attitudes. For this reason, voters have a new view of the people running for presidency.

On the other hand, a candidate can launch a series of negative ad campaigns against a rival. Here, the campaign seeks to degrade voters' perception of an opponent instead of highlighting positive aspects and personal strengths of the sponsoring candidate.

There are two common types of negative ad peddling- attack and contrast. While an attack ad exposes a rival's negativity, a contrast one discusses the sponsor's positive points against a rival's negative points.

1988 (Bush I vs. Dukakis)

The 1988 Presidential election happened when then President Ronald Reagan was just about to retire. It featured Vice President George Bush of the Republican Party and Massachusetts Governor Michael Dukakis of the Democratic Party. Today, the campaign stands out arguably as having the most negative ads in the history of American politics.

In reference to George Bush's rivals, political analysts referred to these men as "the seven dwarfs."

Along with Michael Dukakis, these were Al Gore, Joe Biden, Bruce Babbitt, Richard Gephardt, Paul Simon, and Jesse Jackson.

When campaigning, Bush's camp used television advertising to paint a picture of Michael Dukakis as a liberal politician. For example, they attacked Dukakis's earlier opposition of the mandatory recitation of America's Pledge of Allegiance in US schools.

Before Dukakis had time to respond to the negative attack, the Bush campaign released another one. They accused him of being a member of the ACLU movement and that he carried his membership card wherever he went. Dukakis had actually made this statement in an earlier campaign stop. In response, he said that he was a proud liberal and that he thought the phrase was not abusive.

Further, Bush scoffed at Dukakis for having attended Swarthmore College, a private liberal arts institution in Pennsylvania. He said that Dukakis's views on foreign policy were born in a boutique. In an interview, Maureen Dowd, a columnist for the New York

Times asked Bush if that was a case of the pot calling the kettle black, in reference to Bush's attendance of the Yale University. Bush answered that while his college admitted elite students, he connected with the financial challenges that ordinary Americans faced.

On another negative attack, this time from the Dukakis campaign, television ads seemed to implicate Bush in a number of scandals in the Reagan administration. The campaign stated that Bush was not fit for the highest office because as a powerful Vice President, he had almost the same influence as the aging President Ronald Reagan.

One of these controversies is the Iran-Contra scandal that happened during Reagan's second term. It stated that senior government officials had secretly sold firearms to Iran, contrary to the provisions of the international arms embargo. The trade was ostensibly part of negotiations to facilitate the release of seven U.S hostages held by Hezbollah in Lebanon. It also sought to finance the Contras in Nicaragua, the funding of which Congress had previously outlawed.

In an attempt to quell criticism of his ignorance of military matters, Governor Dukakis staged a controversial photo op. In the picture, Dukakis is seen riding atop an M1 Abrams tank just outside a General Dynamics plant. He smiles while wearing a helmet as he waves to the crowd from one of the tank's hatches. His move seemed to mimic Margaret Thatcher's successful PR outing in which she was pictured riding atop a Challenger Tank in 1986.

Famous photo of Candidate Michael Dukakis in tank.

In the end, Dukakis's photo op proved a massive public relations mistake as his camp received widespread backlash. Many people mocked it and political commentators famously referred to it as "Dukakis in the

---

[37] By http://digitaljournalist.org/issue0309/images/life/dukakis.jpg, Fair use, https://en.wikipedia.org/w/index.php?curid=3616570

tank."

On the other side, Republican nominee, Bush had chosen a young man to be his running mate Senator Dan Quayle (Indiana) ostensibly to appeal to a younger electorate. Senator John McCain quipped that the running mate was so handsome that he would actually have a big impact.

As Quayle was not a seasoned politician, the Democratic campaign alleged that it was dangerous for America to have him as the President's deputy. In his defense, Quayle compared himself to former Senator John F. Kennedy who was also a young political rookie when he successfully ran for presidency. Quayle was 'taken down' infamously during a Vice Presidential debate with Democrat Lloyd Benson.

In yet another negative attack, Donna Brazile, the Democratic Field Director, spread allegations that Republican candidate Bush had a sexual affair with Jennifer Fitzgerald, his assistant. As the allegations were found to be mere rumors, Dukakis fired her.

Later, the Bush campaign derided Dukakis for his failure to prevent pollution of the environment in Boston Harbor. This ad along with others, notably the "Revolving Door" ad, badly hurt Dukakis's chances of being elected president. In the "Revolving Door" ad, the sponsors claimed that Dukakis would allow convicts to walk free in America if he was elected president. One convict featured was Willie Horton. "Whether you were white or black, or red or yellow, Willie Horton was your worst nightmare."[38] As Governor, Michael Dukakis supported opening up the prison letting Willie Horton out for a weekend furlough. Nine times he came back. The 10th time he escaped to Maryland and tortured a young man and raped his wife.

Other accusations about Dukakis were that his wife had burned an American flag and that he had sought treatment for a mental problem.

Outcome of the negative ads

Even as Dukakis performed well in the initial

---

[38] Simon, Roger (November 11, 1990)."How A Murderer And Rapist Became The Bush Campaign's Most Valuable Player". *The Baltimore Sun.*

presidential debate, his negative ads did nothing to deflate Bush's bandwagon. By the time the election rolled around, Bush's bare knuckled attacks had done their damage. A Gallup opinion poll gave Bush a 49-43 lead going into final presidential polls before the election. He did even better when the final votes were cast.

On November 8, 1988, voters went to the ballot. Bush garnered 48.8 million votes against Dukakis's 41.8 million in the popular vote. In the Electoral College, Bush collected an impressive 426 votes against Dukakis's 111.

After Bush was declared America's, 41st President, Dukakis claimed that his own failure to counterattack Bush's negative ads cost him the presidency. Further, he said that his official duties as Governor of Massachusetts barred him from campaigning as effectively as he had wished. While his post-election analysis might hold some truth, one thing is clear- the negative ads sponsored by the Republican Party effectively destroyed Dukakis's presidential ambitions.

RESULTS

1988	Winner	Loser
Nominee	George H. W. Bush	Michael Dukakis
Party	Republican	Democratic
Home State	Texas	Massachusetts
Electoral Votes	426	111
States Won	40	10
Percentage of Votes Won	53.4%	45.6%
Number of Votes	48,886,097	41,809,074

REFERENCES

The Living Room Candidate – Commercials – 1988 – Tank Ride.Livingroomcandidate.org. Online. Retrieved May 11, 2016. http://www.livingroomcandidate.org/commercials

Presidential Elections Vide – Tank Ride.History.com. Online. Retrieved May 11, 2016. http://www.history.com/topics/us-presidents/presidential-elections/videos/tank-ride Geer, John G.

The News Media and the Rise of Negativity in Presidential Campaigns. PS: Political Science & Politics APSC 45, no. 03 (February 2012): 422-27. Online. Retrieved May 11, 2016. doi:10.1017/s1049096512000491

Ridout, T. N. and Franz, M. M. (2011). The Persuasive Power of Campaign Advertising. Philadelphia: Temple University Press. Retrieved May 19, 2016 from http://www.jstor.org/stable/j.ctt14bt9nv

Dionne, E. J. Junior. (November 9, 1988). The 1988 Elections; Bush is elected by a 6-5 margin with solid G.O.P. base in south. Democrats hold both houses How poll was taken. New York: The New York Times. Retrieved May 19, 2016 from http://www.nytimes.com/1988/11/09/us/1988-elections-bush-elected-6-5-margin-with-solid-gop-base-south-democrats-hold.html?pagewanted=all

Van der Meer, J. (June 29, 2012). Negative advertising in U.S. presidential elections: "as American as Mississippi mud". A graduate thesis from the University of Amsterdam. Retrieved May 19, 2016 from http://dare.uva.nl/cgi/arno/show.cgi?fid=449978

Morrison, D. (n.d.). United States Presidential Election of 1988. Online: Encyclopaedia Britannica. Retrieved May 19, 2016 from http://www.britannica.com/event/United-States-presidential-election-of-1988

2004

CHAPTER 11: Post 9/11 Battle

GEORGE W. BUSH VS. JOHN KERRY

George H. Bush

John Kerry

The 55th United States quadrennial presidential election was held on 2nd November 2004. Republican George W. Bush won the election with 50.7% of the vote earning 286 electoral votes and winning 31 states. His main challenger was Democratic Candidate John Kerry.

It is an undeniable fact that television ads are an integral part of the American experience; they're ubiquitous, glaring, pushy, and oftentimes over the top, but in the end, it's impossible to imagine modern-day America without those special two minutes in between crowd favorites like football and soap TV dramas. It's a shame, then, that the combination between the all-American tradition of advertising and the even more all-American tradition of presidential elections combine to form such a horrendous slurry of hate and purported debauchery, both given and taken.

Aggressive Beginning

Almost a year before the 2004 presidential elections, seated president George W. Bush blasted into the television scene with ads that tore down his competition, spending over $40,000,000 on campaign ads before most other presidents in the past had even considered going on the campaign trail. This was an unprecedented move, one that would have repercussions for the entirety of the election process following the campaign. Kerry was depicted in these ads as being a weak president, incapable of battling terrorism, soft on hard issues that mattered to Americans, and a general all-around unfit person for the office of the head of state. Because not many people knew of Kerry at the time of the ad campaign, Bush was able to shape public opinion without interference from the other side—this was a shot in just the right place to prime the country for an election filled with hate speech, denunciations, and general foolishness that was completely unsuited to the high ideals of the American presidential election.

Counter Attacks

Several months later, after Kerry had earned the Democratic nomination, he began to counter attack Bush playing ads that questioned where Bush's budget deficits had really come from, questioning whether or not it was right to have a president that was kept up in office with high approval ratings for the sole reason that he was there to console the nation after the horrific September 11th attacks.

It was those attacks that would be the key to victory, and it was those attacks that were exploited for the sole purpose of showing power, with both sides making accusations against each other with. The September 11th attacks were changed from being something horrible that the entire nation could get behind into ammunition and fodder for both sides to throw at each other. Never mind the fact that more than two thousand Americans died in the attack; never mind the fact that some of America's greatest symbols of peace and prosperity were destroyed. As long as it fit in the cannon, and as long as it played on the heart strings of the public, the two presidential candidates would fire it at each other like an old Civil War era cannon ball.

The Role of the Internet

The Internet also played a huge role in the 2004 campaigns, with blogging and commenting being some of the main communication forums where attacks took place, where people were able to fight it out anonymously which led to more brash and harsh battles than had the antagonists been face to face.

Not being Internet savvy probably cost Kerry the victory—he only stepped up his campaigns Internet marketing halfway through his presidential campaign, whereas Bush already had developed a strong online presence. Kerry would have done well to learn from fellow Democrat Howard Dean who is credited with pioneering Internet-based fundraising and who actually led all Democratic Candidates in 2004 due to a large extent to his use of social media in the pre-Facebook era prior to the Iowa Caucus.

It's a now-obvious fact that when people talk politics on the Internet, they typically aren't nice. However, what isn't obvious is the fact that the Internet facilitates the percolation of ideas through other means than direct conversion the Internet influencing how others think and behave. Thus the battle between Kerry and Bush became the first battle for the hearts and minds of voters using the Internet.

When the first ever television debate was shown between Kennedy and Nixon in 1960, there was a split in the perspective of people who had either seen the broadcast on TV or listened to it on the radio; it's arguable that that day was the day when the presidential election turned from a contest between wits—being more like an ancient Grecian forum—into a popularity contest that mirrors those found in high school prom king and queen races. The Bush vs Kerry debacle was merely an evolution of what had been happening for more than forty years, and what is still happening today. The popularization of mass media, the invention of television, of the Internet, and the rising cost of advertising to a larger audience has brought the electoral process to its knees in terms of 'reality,' a term that is used loosely to indicate what is really best for the country.

Today's Campaigns

Nowadays, it's not uncommon for people to vote for their president not based on their policy or their track record, but rather based on the suit that they wore to a debate, or on the facial expressions that the candidates exhibited during speeches. The world has become more consumptive, more passive, and as a result, elections have gone from being a foundation stone upon which the United States was based, to being simple contests that gauge how well each candidate trashes the other and makes their own face seem more palatable to the viewers, most of whom are participating in the debauchery themselves. The presidential election process has changed a lot in the past half-century, and while some changes may make for a better country, others have deepened the dark and sinister underside that has arisen out of the necessity to appeal to basic human psychology above reason and logic.

RESULTS

2004	Winner	Loser
Nominee	George W. Bush	John Kerry
Party	Republican	Democratic
Home State	Texas	Massachusetts
Electoral Votes	286	251
States Won	31	19
Percentage of Votes Won	50.7%	48.3%
Number of Votes	62,040,610	59,028,444

REFERENCES

Cornfield, M. (2005, March 6). Commentary on the impact of the Internet on the 2004 election. Online. Retrieved from http://www.pewInternet.org/2005/03/06/commentary-on-the-impact-of-the-Internet-on-the-2004-election/

West, D. M. (n.d.). The Bush versus Kerry Air War. Online. Retrieved from http://www.insidepolitics.org/heard/WestReport504.html

QUESTIONS & EXERCISES

These are meant to stimulate conversation in classes, for clubs, for groups of interested citizens, or for people with a natural curiosity about politics in general and the American Presidential Election process specifically.

Questions:

1. Does negative campaigning work?

2. What evidence can you find to support this?

3. Is it fair that the electoral college actually determines the winner? Why or why not? Is there a better system for selecting a winner?

4. What role to Political Action Committees play in influencing the outcomes of campaigns?

5. How do governments enable or limit negative campaigning?

6. Does a multiparty system lead to more or less negative campaigning?

7. Can positive campaigning be just as affective? What proof do you have?

8. A variety of sources are used in compiling these essays. What sources would you use and how could you verify their accuracy? Does it matter?

Exercises:

1. Pick a political campaign. Analyze and then summarize the tone of the campaign. Was it positive or negative? What specific things suggest this?

2. Based on your research, which US presidential campaign was the most positive? What was the result? Provide evidence to support your position.

3. How does the media influence the tone of a campaign? What research supports your position? How has this evolved over time?

4. Compare campaigns in two different countries. Identify the timeline and process for selecting a new leader (President, Prime Minister as common global examples). Then identify how the candidates communicate with potential voters. What can you conclude from this comparison?

5. Draw a timeline identifying the major negative campaign tactics used. Then write a brief essay discussing the impact these tactics had on the outcome of the campaign.

6. Draw a timeline of the evolution of the media and its role in presidential elections. Then write a brief essay discussing how media and its role in presidential elections has evolved over time.

ABOUT THE AUTHOR

Graham W. Milton Jr. is an educator, an entrepreneur, and a writer who loves to travel, to hike, and to read about other people. He has voted in every Presidential election and most other elections since he turned 18. An explorer by nature, his views on politics – like many things, continue to evolve as he continues on his own personal journey.